THE MAN FOR THE DAY

J. Josh Smith

The Man for the Day

Answering the Call to Godly Manhood

B&H Publishing®
Brentwood, Tennessee

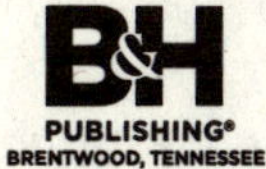

979-8-3845-1960-7

Published by B&H Publishing Group
Brentwood, Tennessee

Dewey Decimal Classification: 248.842
Subject Heading: MEN / CHRISTIAN LIFE / CHARACTER

Cover design and illustrations by João Neves of Good Illustration LTD. Author photo(s) by Mathew Perkins.

1 2 3 4 5 6 7 • 29 28 27 26

To two men who have been "the
man for the day" in my life:

Barry St. Clair and Fred Hartley

From the start of my journey with Jesus until now, no two men have set the trajectory of my life more than you. You have not only pointed me in the right direction, you have walked with me and loved me like a father with a son. Your influence on me is immeasurable—and so is my love and gratitude.

Acknowledgments

THE CONTENT FOR this book came out of an extended study on the life of Elijah with the men who attend the monthly men's breakfast at Prince Avenue Baptist Church. To those men, thank you for your presence, responsiveness, and encouragement. I love our time together!

Jason Duesing, I would have never started writing if you had not encouraged me to do so. Thank you for your belief and friendship over the past twenty-five years. You remain a dear brother.

Logan Pyron, you worked through this book at a very difficult time in your life, yet you gave it so much thought and attention. Your help and excitement has blessed me greatly. Thank you!

Erik Wolgemuth, I had no idea how much better you would make this journey. What a joy to work with you! Thank you, brother.

Nathan Lino and Kevin Ueckert, your genuine friendship is one of the greatest gifts in my life. I could never thank you enough.

Steven Smith, I was writing this book while you were going through an incredibly difficult season. Watching your perseverance, faith, joy, and optimism inspired every word. I'm "actually" very thankful for your friendship.

Andrea, Lily, Gracie, Josie, Annie, and Josiah, you have made home my favorite place to be. I love you.

Contents

Introduction

The Man for the Day

FOR MOST OF my adult life, I have read a biography every January, and I have been inspired by the lives of many incredible men and women. If I had to choose my Mount Rushmore of spiritual leaders from church history, it would be difficult to narrow it down to only four. But one figure I would be certain to choose is the large, familiar, bearded, and seemingly kind face of Charles Spurgeon.

Spurgeon most famously built and pastored the Metropolitan Tabernacle Church in London in the mid-1800s. He preached the gospel to more than a million people and personally baptized more than fifteen thousand new believers. Spurgeon's impact on his generation was massive, and nearly one hundred and fifty years later, he remains one of the most widely read and quoted pastors in church history.

Although Spurgeon has a long list of accomplishments, his most enduring contribution has been his God-centered, Christ-exalting, white-hot preaching. I wish, just once, I could have been one of the six thousand people who gathered at the Tabernacle each week to hear him preach. And if I had to pick a Sunday, I would go with February 5, 1888.

On that Sunday, Spurgeon preached a sermon from Revelation 2:12–13 titled, "Holding Fast the Faith."[1] This is one of the few Spurgeon sermons I've revisited multiple times. Every time I read it, I can sense the fire in his bones, the passion in his heart, the strength of his voice, and the anointing of the Holy Spirit. Every time I read it, the heat in his heart spreads to mine.

He begins the sermon by painting an incredible picture of Jesus in Revelation 2. It's a picture of Jesus as a "man of war" holding "a sharp sword with two edges," defending His church and leading them into certain victory. About this he says:

> His sword is for the defense of the faithful. It is drawn from its sheath to protect the timid and the trembling. Jesus is come as our Joshua, to chase the enemy before us, and lead us onward, conquering and to conquer. The sword with two edges is the defender of the least of those whose hearts are right before the Lord.[2]

It's hard for me to stay seated when I read that.

The real goal of the sermon, however, was not to paint a picture of this "man of war," but to call the church to *follow* this "man of war" with purity, faith, and courage, to "hold fast the faith in the teeth of opposition." To this he said:

> If in the heat of the battle our good name or our life must be risked to win the victory, then let us say, "In this battle some of us must fall; why should not I? I will take part and lot with my Master, and bear reproach for his sake." Only brave soldiers are worthy of our great Lord. Those who sneak into the rear, that they may be comfortable, are not worthy of the kingdom. What will our Captain say of cowards in that day when he distributes rewards to his faithful ones? Brethren, we must be willing to bear ridicule for Christ's sake, even that peculiarly envenomed ridicule which "the culture" are so apt to pour upon us. We must be willing to be thought great fools for Jesus' sake.[3]

In the final point of his sermon, he urges the church to hold fast to the name and faith of Jesus. It is a call to hold tightly to the faith, love the faith, and defend the faith. He then reminds his listeners of those who had given so much to ensure that the faith was passed on to us. To the men who "loved the faith and the name of Jesus too well to see them trampled on," he said:

> Personally, when my bones have been tortured with rheumatism, I have remembered Job Spurgeon, doubtless of my own stock, who in Chelmsford Jail

> was allowed a chair, because he could not lie down by reason of rheumatic pain. That Quaker's broadbrim overshadows my brow. Perhaps I inherit his rheumatism; but that I do not regret if I have his stubborn faith, which will not let me yield a syllable of the truth of God. When I think of how others have suffered for the faith, a little scorn or unkindness seems a mere trifle, not worthy of mention. An ancestry of lovers of the faith ought to be a great plea with us to abide by the Lord God of our fathers, and the faith in which they lived. As for me, I must hold the old gospel: I can do no other. God helping me, I will endure the consequences of what men think obstinacy.[4]

Even though every line of the sermon seems worthy to be underlined and quoted, like any good preacher, he leaves the best for last. He ends the sermon with these words that will make any Christian man with a heartbeat and an ounce of God's Spirit ready to charge the gates of hell for the cause of Christ. When talking about the legacy of faithful men who have gone before us he says:

> These men loved the faith and the name of Jesus too well to see them trampled on. Note what we owe them, and let us pay to our sons the debt we owe our fathers. It is today as it was in the Reformers' days. Decision is needed. Here is the day for the

man, where is the man for the day? We who have had the gospel passed to us by martyr hands dare not trifle with it, nor sit by and hear it denied by traitors, who pretend to love it, but inwardly abhor every line of it. . . . Look you, sirs, there are ages yet to come. If the Lord does not speedily appear, there will come another generation, and another, and all these generations will be tainted and injured if we are not faithful to God and to his truth to-day. We have come to a turning-point in the road. If we turn to the right, mayhap our children and our children's children will go that way; but if we turn to the left, generations yet unborn will curse our names for having been unfaithful to God and to his Word. I charge you, not only by your ancestry, but by your posterity, that you seek to win the commendation of your Master, that though you dwell where Satan's seat is, you yet hold fast his name, and do not deny his faith. God grant us faithfulness, for the sake of the souls around us! How is the world to be saved if the church is false to her Lord? How are we to lift the masses if our fulcrum is removed? If our gospel is uncertain, what remains but increasing misery and despair? Stand fast, my beloved, in the name of God! I, your brother in Christ, entreat you to abide in the truth. Quit yourselves like men,

> be strong. The Lord sustain you for Jesus' sake.
>
> Amen.[5]

I not only feel the passion in his heart and the fire in his bones, I feel those same things stirred up in me. His words make me long to be the man God has called me to be and make me long to call on a new generation of men to faithfully follow Jesus Christ, the man of war, into battle. His words make me want to leave a life of unholy contentment and strive to fulfill everything God wants from me. If his words do any of the same things in your heart, this book is for you.

The Day for the Man

I first read the last paragraph of this Spurgeon sermon in a book titled *The Forgotten Spurgeon* by Iain Murray. I was twenty-two years old, single, and a full-time missionary in the central European country of Slovakia. I was sitting in a small café when the Lord used those words of Spurgeon to light a fire in my heart. Over the years, there have been times in which that fire has raged like an uncontrollable blaze. At other times, I've only felt the warmth of a small ember. But more than twenty-five years later, the fire ignited by Spurgeon's words has not gone out.

The spark the Lord used to start that fire came from one simple statement and one simple question hidden toward the end of his sermon. One statement and one question from one sermon preached more than 130 years ago has been a continual source of passion, pushing me to be the man God wants me to be. The question is this: "Here is the day for the man, where is the man for the day?"[6]

Spurgeon felt the need for faithful men. Men who take up the mantle passed down from the martyrs who had gone before them. Men who have suffered greatly to ensure the next generation heard the gospel. He looked at his generation and saw the desperate need for these men. "Here is the day for the man," he said.[7]

Don't you feel the same thing? Don't you feel how desperately we need godly, faithful, strong, courageous, self-sacrificing, Spirit-filled men? Don't you look around and wonder where the men are who have the backbone and resolve to stand against culture pressures for the faith passed down to us? Don't you feel that now is the day for the man?

I recently met with a man who worked for a Christian publisher. He told me that women's Bible studies are what kept them in business. That's what pays the bills. And historically, Bible studies and books for men don't sell. But this publisher told me they are starting to see a rise in requests for men's books. He asked me if I knew why.

I don't know all the reasons men are starting to buy more books and do more Bible studies specifically for them, but the more I've thought about it, a few things become clear.

First, pastors are realizing that they cannot ignore men any longer. They know the men in their church are dying, and they need help. They are also realizing that silly, trite, and shallow programs will not suffice to create the men we desperately need.

Second, men are feeling the depths of their own deficiencies. As I minister to the men in the church where I pastor and to men around the country, I sense more and more how much men feel defeated, discouraged, and even displaced. They are tired of feeling that way. They want to be faithful, godly men, but they don't know where to start.

More than all of that, there is a growing desire among men to stand against the cultural insanity of the day, fight the besetting sins of the day, and be genuinely used by God. Men are tired of feeling defeated, being scolded, and watching their families, churches, and culture be attacked. They are tired of feeling like it's wrong to be a strong man. In other words, men are feeling fed up! They see the need for men, and they want to be the man God has called them to be.

The Man for the Day

Spurgeon's statement resonates with us: "Here is the day for the man." But it's his question that must motivate us: "Where is the man for the day?"[8]

We all know men who like to rant about every cultural problem, societal need, and spiritual deficiency, and yet never do anything about it. It's like their spiritual gift is identifying things others should be doing better. The reality is we are all pretty good at that. Still, we must resist this temptation when it comes to the need for men. We must not just identify the need; we must meet the need. We must commit ourselves to becoming the man for the day.

This book is written out of the conviction that now is the day for the man. This book is also written as a road map for how you can become "the man for the day." What does it mean to be the man for the day?

The man for the day is a man who is ready and willing to be used by God when, where, and how God desires to use him.

In my book *The Titus Ten*, I wrote that every man has four primary domains. There are four areas in which every man must be sacrificially committed to work. Those four areas are (1) his own flesh, (2) his local church, (3) his family, and (4) his workplace. Those are every man's four primary domains.[9]

The man for the day knows the areas in which God has called him and then faithfully, courageously, sacrificially, and consistently seeks to do everything God has called him to do in each of those areas. The man for the day does not just see the need; he meets the need.

The man for the day is a man who loves God, hears from God, and walks in obedience to God. He is a man who has surrendered his life to be and do everything God has called him to. He is a man who wants nothing more than to fulfill every good work God has laid out for him to accomplish.

Elijah: The Man for His Day

A few years ago, I decided to start walking through the life of Elijah at our church's monthly men's breakfast. I love the life and ministry of Elijah. I was eager to dig deeper into his life and thought that I could at least spend five or six weeks on him. I finished twenty-three months later, and still didn't feel like I did him justice.

There was a desperate need for godly men in Elijah's day. Elijah was the man for the day. There was a time in his life when he thought he was the only one. And although his life is remarkable and inimitable in many ways, he shows us how to be the man for the day. Not only because of his strengths but because of his weaknesses, both of which, thankfully, are recorded for us.

As we walk through his life, we will see the ten marks of becoming the kind of men we need and need to be. Elijah will not only equip us but he will motivate us, encourage us, and inspire us to be "the man for the day."

Do Small Things for God

When I was young, people often used to say, "God is going to do great things with you someday." I don't think this was because they sensed some special anointing on my life as a ten-year-old boy. I think part of this was because of the family in which I was raised and some of my natural personality.

It was kind of people to say that. They said it with great intentions. They intended for it to bless me. But over time, those statements led to more defeat than victory. When I thought about "great things," I thought about Hudson Taylor, George Müller, Adoniram Judson, and Billy Graham. This meant, in my mind, if I didn't end up doing the things they did, I had failed to do great things for God.

It took me a long time to get free from those expectations. It took many years of frustration, angst, disappointment, and unfulfilled hopes. It took me dying to the unrealistic expectations others had put on me and I had put on myself. It took a season of painful but necessary suffering and death to self. It was a painful process, but one that changed my life.

At the end of that process, I came to a place where I genuinely wanted to do nothing more than love my family, lead and pastor the church God had entrusted to me, love and serve those around me, and not care if anyone outside of that circle ever knew who I was. Even as I write those words, I still feel the joy and freedom of that.

Although our guide through this journey is the greatest prophet of the Old Testament, this book is not designed to create "great men of God" in the way we often interpret it. This book is designed to help *you* be the man that God has created and called *you* to be. Not comparing yourself to anyone else. Not competing with other men. Not coveting the success of others. But to simply be ready and willing, every day, and every moment, in every area, to fulfill God's calling for you.

This is a book about doing small things for God. It's about winning the day. It's about faithfully fulfilling what God has for you today, knowing that those who are faithful in little can be entrusted with more. This is a book about being the man for the day—and the day is today.

Although we certainly need "men for the day" in politics and in the pulpit, what we really need is more of these men in homes, churches, communities, and workplaces. We need men who are not looking to be known but are looking to be used. We are looking for men who just want to be who God has called them to be—nothing more and nothing less.

A Beginning Prayer

A few years ago, someone challenged me to write down one prayer that summarized what I wanted God to do in my life, and then pray it every day. I liked that idea. It sounded simple. It also sounded helpful.

As I began to work on that prayer I found it more difficult than I imagined, but ultimately more helpful than I imagined. It was really challenging to summarize what I really wanted to see God do. But as the Lord gave me clarity, it became not only a statement of longing and desire for what I wanted God to do, but a way to keep me focused on being the man I wanted to be.

In that prayer, I have a few lines that have been so life-giving to me. These lines flow out of the death of my desire to do "great things for God" and the birth of my desire to do exactly what God has for me—whether the world views that as great or not.

One part of my daily prayer says this: "Lord, I surrender myself fully to You. I only want for my life what You want for my life. Nothing more and nothing less. Please fulfill every desire you have for me. I don't want to miss a thing."

Those lines have been more life-giving to me than you can imagine. They motivate me to be all that God wants me to be and also free me from trying to be something other than what God wants. I want to encourage you to stop and pray that prayer. And consider making it the prayer you pray throughout this journey.

As we begin this road map for becoming "the man for the day," we begin with surrender. The place we must start. And we begin with a genuine heart-cry to God that He would make each one of us into the man that He has created us to be—the man for the day. May it be each one of us.

Chapter 1

Surrender

Surrender: Submitting your will to the will of God and trusting Him to write your story.

IT WAS JULY 9, 2013. I only remember that date because two days later our family would experience something that would change our lives forever. I was the camp pastor at a student camp in central Texas. My role was to preach every morning and be available to counsel every night.

On Tuesday night, I sat and listened as a well-known student evangelist preached a message calling students to surrender everything to Jesus. He called them to trust Jesus with everything, and as a response to that trust, willingly surrender complete control and authority to Him.

At the end of his sermon, he asked if students would be willing to pray a simple prayer of full surrender to Jesus. He didn't give them words to pray; he just asked them to pray. Students all over the room got on their knees and surrendered their lives completely to Jesus.

Many students walked toward counselors for prayer. That is why I was in the room.

But as I watched God work inside these students, something unexpected was happening in me. I was scared. I was beyond scared. I was almost terrified. I was terrified at the thought of what it would mean for my life, my family, my church, my health, or my career if I surrendered everything to the Lord. This came out of nowhere. I had heard countless sermons on surrender. I had preached countless sermons on surrender. But for some reason, at that moment, I feared what it would mean for me to surrender.

I am fully confident that at that time I had a genuine relationship with Jesus and was actively trusting and following Him. I had not only surrendered my life to Christ but had surrendered to the ministry. Yet for some reason, in that moment, it felt more difficult than it ever had.

As students walked forward, I slipped out the back. I went to my room and wrestled with God. I will never forget that night. I paced, knelt, cried out, and laid face down on the ground. At some point in the middle of the night, I fell asleep. The next morning, I woke up to an unexpected call telling me I needed to come home. I got in the car and continued my wrestling match with God. I still could not pray a prayer of surrender.

In those moments, all alone in the car, the Lord reminded me of a little phrase from 1 John 4:18. Over and over again, I just kept hearing the words, "Perfect love casts out fear. . . . Perfect love casts out fear. . . . Perfect love casts out fear" (ESV). In those moments I realized the only reason I would be afraid to surrender is if I questioned God's love. If I trusted His heart, I could trust Him with my life.

Somewhere on Highway 175 going west toward Dallas, Texas, with a new confidence in God's love for me, I told the Lord that I surrendered everything to Him.

As I look back on that moment, I realize what Jacob must have realized when he looked back on wrestling all night with God in Genesis 32: God always wrestles with us to prepare us. And that is exactly what was happening to me. God was preparing me for something. God was calling me into a greater awareness of His love because God was preparing me for something that would demand it. He was preparing me for something that demanded surrender. A new work of God always demands a new surrender to God.

A Needed Man

The story of 1 and 2 Kings is a sad one. It shouldn't have been, but it was. These two books follow the story of the kings who led God's people after the death of King David.

When David died, the kingdom was filled with great hope and expectations. David's son Solomon became king. He famously asked the Lord for wisdom, and the Lord gave it to him. With that wisdom he built the temple that his father, David, longed to see built—and it was magnificent. When the temple was dedicated, God showed up. The people worshiped, God was glorified, and it appeared as if this was the beginning of something wonderful.

But Solomon's heart turned away from God. He was ruled by his own passions, not God's. He married foreign women, built unholy alliances, and allowed the worship of pagan gods. And as is always the case, his sin was not just his problem. His sin led the nation into a devastating spiral of idolatry, rebellion, and immorality.

After Solomon's death, his two sons battled for the kingdom. This resulted in the division of the kingdom into two kingdoms: the northern kingdom of Israel and the southern kingdom of Judah. These two books are titled "Kings" because they follow the story—the mostly sad story—of the thirty-nine kings of these two kingdoms.

Out of those thirty-nine kings, there were four who did right in the eyes of the Lord. Four. The other thirty-five were evil. And all four good kings were from the southern kingdom. The northern kingdom did not have one—not one—good king. Out of eighteen kings, they did not have one good one.[1]

Jeroboam, the first king in the north, became the prototype of evil kings. The worst kings are known as kings "like Jeroboam." Ultimately, the Lord took him out and another king took the throne. From there, the story just keeps getting worse. Try to follow this:

- Jeroboam was followed by Nadab. Nadab reigned two years, did evil in the sight of the Lord, and was assassinated by a man named Baasha.
- Baasha's first act as king was to murder everyone from the house of his predecessor. He

reigned for twenty-four years, did what was evil, and died.

- Baasha's son Elah became king. After reigning for two years, while in a drunken stupor, he was murdered by his servant Zimri.
- Zimri became king and immediately killed everyone in Elah's family. He did not leave one of Elah's male relatives or friends alive. Zimri's rule, although busy, did not last long. He was king for seven days before committing suicide by burning down the house he was inside.
- After a brief civil war, Zimri was followed by Omri. He reigned for twelve years, and in those twelve years managed to do "more evil than all who were before him" (1 Kings 16:25).
- After Omri's death, his son Ahab became king. Ahab, we are told, did more evil and more to provoke the Lord to anger than any other king before him (1 Kings 16:29–34). That is saying a lot. But much like Solomon, his worst decision was marrying a pagan wife. He married Jezebel, the daughter of a pagan king, who not only led the nation into the worship of her god, Baal, but worked to rid the land of every prophet of the Lord.

Just one hundred years after King David's death, the nation of Israel was in a state of absolute moral chaos. Under the rule of King Ahab, new temples to false gods were constructed on every hillside, while the Lord's prophets were being gathered and killed. It's a sad story. It's also a good reminder: Nothing causes more damage to a family, a church, or a nation than ungodly men.

If there was ever a "day for the man,"[2] this was it. In the presence of these ungodly men, God was about to raise up a man. This is what God does. When there needs to be a man for the day, God raises him up and calls him out. As the story continues, we get an even more important reminder: Nothing causes more good to a family, a church, or a nation than godly men.

An Obscure Man

In the midst of the spiral of moral chaos, an obscure prophet by the name of Elijah comes out of nowhere as if he was shot out of a carnival cannon.

We know almost nothing about him. We don't know about his family, his training, or his background. All we know is from a half-sentence introduction of him that says, "Now Elijah the Tishbite, from the Gilead settlers . . ." (1 Kings 17:1). That's it. That's our introduction to the greatest prophet of the Old Testament. It's not much, but it's enough to get a good picture in our minds.

Elijah was a Tishbite. Tishbe was a small, obscure town in Gilead. Gilead was a place known for its rugged, outdoorsy, hardworking, farming people. Elijah was not refined. His hands were not soft. His neck was not pale. His clothes were not new. He was not unfamiliar with long days and hard work. He was a simple, strong, hardworking, God-fearing outdoorsman.

Centuries later, John the Baptist would give us a little clue to what Elijah might have looked like. When John the Baptist came on the scene with his rough robe, loud voice, and strange diet, looking like he always slept outside, the people thought he was Elijah (John 1:21).

But the most important detail is not his looks, but his name. His name is more than just a name. His name is his calling card. His name tells us who he was, why he'd come, and what was most important to him.

The ancient Hebrew name for God is El, as in Elohim. Elijah's name starts with that. The "i" after "El" is a first-person possessive pronoun. The "jah" represents the personal name of God, Yahweh; the covenant name of God—the name that God gave to His people. So Elijah's name is made up of two names for God and a personal possessive pronoun. In other words, Elijah's name meant, "My God is the Lord." Or to say it another way, "I'm God's man."[3]

Depending on how you look at it, this is either a perfect name for the moment or a terrible name for the moment. I don't know if his parents gave him this name or if the Lord changed his name, but either way, his name made a statement. A strong statement. Especially in an age in which all of God's men were being killed. Elijah's name was a statement of rebellion against everything happening in the culture around him.

The lack of detail about his life might make him an obscure man, but his name made him a surrendered man.

A Surrendered Man

Fulfilling the role of a faithful prophet, Elijah's first words were God's words. And they weren't easy words. The very first thing Elijah did was stand before King Ahab and say, "As the LORD, the God of Israel lives, before whom I stand, surely there shall be neither dew nor rain these years, except by my word" (17:1b ESV).

What was so bad about that? Well, if there was no rain, there would be no crops. If there were no crops, there would be no food. If there was no food, the people would starve. These were words of judgment. God was judging the people for their continual rebellion. But they were not only words of judgment; they were also words of grace. The pigsty was not only judgment on the prodigal son's rebellion, but it was also a call to come home (Luke 15:11–32). The lack of rain was not only God's judgment on His people, but a call for them to repent and come home.

This was not an easy message to hear, and it was definitely not an easy message to deliver. But Elijah, without any hesitation or reservation, without any fear or fanfare, came on the scene with nothing but a word from God.

Standing before the king with a word of judgment is an act of incredible courage (which we will discuss later). But his name reminds us that his courage flowed from something deeper. His name shows us the foundation from which his courage was built.

Elijah's name tells us, first and foremost, that Elijah was a surrendered man. He was God's man. He was not controlled by anyone else but God. He could not be bought because he had already been bought. He said what God said, no matter the cost, because he had already surrendered his mouth to the Lord. He went wherever he was called to go, no matter the cost, because he had already surrendered his feet to the Lord. This surrender, above everything else, would be the primary mark of his remarkable life.

Elijah came out of nowhere, in the midst of a perverse, godless society that hated God, and said, "I'm God's man!"

The reason we are studying the life of Elijah is because he was the man for the day. He was ready and willing to do whatever God called him to do. But the reason he was the man for the day is because he was God's man. And he was God's man because he was a surrendered man. He was not trying to write his own story; he was trusting God to write his story.

He was willing to stand alone. He was willing to suffer. He was willing to die. He was willing to say the hard things to the hardest people. He was willing to be confrontational and even willing to be obscure. And that resonates with us. We want to be that kind of man.

And it all begins with a surrendered life. Before Elijah stood in front of King Ahab and said, "I'm God's man," he had already knelt before his King and said, "God, I'm Your man."

Being the man for the day is about being a man who is ready and willing to be used when, where, and how God desires to use you. This means being the man for the day begins with trusting God to call the shots. It's rooted in complete surrender to God. It is not about you being the man you want to be, but being the man God wants you to be. It's not about fulfilling your plans, but God's—no matter what those plans might be. Elijah was a surrendered man. And his surrender was essential to his usefulness. So is ours.

A Life of Surrender

Surrender is a difficult word for men. It goes against everything culture tells us about what makes a man. Cowards surrender. Weak men surrender. We are told to never be anyone else's man but always be our own man.

Surrender is the reason so many men won't give their lives to Christ. Surrender means the loss of control, the loss of ownership, the loss of rights. We don't want to lose control. We don't want to be owned by anyone. We don't want to relinquish our rights. We don't want someone else calling the shots. There may be no word that goes against our cultural idea of manhood more than the word *surrender*.

Dietrich Bonhoeffer famously said, "The cross is laid on every Christian. . . . As we embark upon discipleship we surrender ourselves to Christ in union with his death—we give over our lives to death . . . When Christ calls a man, he bids him come and die."[4] Meaning, the invitation to follow Jesus is an invitation to death. In order to be saved you must be willing to lay down your life in order to gain His (Matt. 16:25). There is no salvation without the willingness to let go of all authority and all rights and surrender yourself completely to the control of Christ.

And here is the beautiful irony—it is in that death to self that we gain life. The abundant life that Jesus promises us only comes through the death that He demands from us (John 10:10). When we lose our life, we actually gain life. The gospel explains why this must be true.

The good news of Jesus Christ is that we are sinners, separated from God because of our sin, and under the just wrath of God (Rom. 3:23). But God, because of His great love and mercy, sent His Son Jesus Christ to live a sinless life and die a criminal's death (Eph. 2:4). His death was not for His sin, but for ours (2 Cor. 5:21). And if we will acknowledge our inability to save ourselves and trust in Jesus alone, calling upon His name and asking Him to save us, we can be saved by His death (Rom. 10:13). But that is not the end. Jesus rose again, defeating death, ensuring that we are not only saved by His death, but receive new, abundant, and eternal life by His resurrection.

And all of this—all of this—being saved from death by His death and gaining abundant life through His Spirit—is ours by grace. Meaning, we can't earn it. In order to receive it, we simply acknowledge that we can't earn it and ask God to give it to us (Eph. 2:8–9).

Life with Jesus begins with this kind of humility. And it is that humility that is at the heart of surrender. Surrender begins when we acknowledge that we need something we don't have. But Jesus has it all. And as you trust and follow Him in the continual process of death to self and resurrection life, God makes you into the man He wants you to be. Primarily, a man who is controlled by His Spirit, not self.

You cannot be the man God has called you to be unless you are first and foremost controlled by the Spirit of God. It is the Spirt that gives life. It is the Spirit that must lead. It is the Spirit that must bear fruit. But the Spirit only fills those who surrender themselves to His control.

Being God's Man

Before Elijah ever came on the scene, he laid down his desires to be his own man and decided to be God's man. It was the foundation of his usefulness. And it will be the foundation of ours as well. The truth is, you can never be God's man unless you are a surrendered man because you can't be your man and God's man at the same time.

This is what we often miss. We miss the truth that life with Jesus is one of continual surrender. It is about dying daily (1 Cor. 15:31). The gospel teaches us that there is no resurrection without death. So, as we die daily and surrender our life to the Lord, then, and only then, will we experience the resurrection life of Jesus and the power of His Spirit.

But let's be clear: Surrender is not just a prayer. Surrender is a work of God's Spirit. Surrender is also a spiritual discipline. It is not just a disposition of the heart; it is an act of the will. It is the discipline of continually surrendering every area of our life to him. *Every* area.

Take your finances, for example. I love to challenge men to give financially. Not only because I know that God blesses it and because God has used it in my life as much as anything, but because it is one of the most basic yet profound acts of surrender. It's one thing to surrender our lives, but it's another thing to surrender our money. Surrender says, "My money is not mine, it's the Lord's." If you are not giving sacrificially and consistently, you are not a surrendered man.

And although this type of complete surrender sounds difficult, it is actually the starting place of true joy. There is incredible freedom in totally entrusting your life to the One who created you, knows you best, loves you most, and has plans for you that you could never imagine. Everything you long for comes from the life of the Spirit in you. And that life only comes to those who are surrendered. If you want to be the man for the day, you must first be God's man. And being God's man is about surrendering your life, over and over again, to Him.

The Rest of the Story

It was July 11, 2013. It was two days after I began to wrestle with God about surrendering my life to Him. It was the day after I finally prayed the words, "Lord, I trust You with my life in every way. Do with me whatever You want to do." On that day, my wife and I walked into a small, dark room filled with computer monitors and listened as the doctor told us that cancer had spread across my wife's body.

She was thirty-two years old with no previous health conditions. At that time, we had four daughters ranging from ages ten to one. The following months would be the hardest months of our lives (the rest of that story is at the end of the book).

As I look back on those difficult days, I now realize they were the starting place of a much greater work of God in my life. I would not be the man I am today if it were not for that experience. I hated it at the time, but I would not trade it for anything. That moment of surrender was preparing me for what God knew was coming. And what was coming was the preparation to mold me into the man I am today.

God knew that I would only be prepared for that season if I was a surrendered man. Why? Because surrender is always the foundation for God's work in us. I needed to settle in my heart that I could trust the Lord no matter what. And that would be manifested by my willingness to surrender my life to Him because I knew how much He loved me and how much better His plans were than mine. God rewards faith, and surrender is our declaration that we trust God to write our story.

I do not tell you that story to scare you. The moment you surrender to the Lord is, hopefully, not also the day you get the worst news of your life. I tell you that story to remind you that surrender is the starting place for a new work of God in your life. It always will be.

You can trust God to write your story. Don't try to write your own. He writes better stories than you ever could. Trust Him to do it. Surrender all you are and all you have to Him.

The Man for the Day

The man for the day wants nothing more than to be God's man, not his own man. He knows he cannot be both, so he fights continually against the desire to take control.

The man for the day surrenders himself daily to the will of God. He knows that surrender is not a one-time occurrence, but a daily necessity. He continually fights the enemies of self-will, self-love, and self-service. He continually looks to the Lord for leadership and wisdom. He wants what God wants.

The man for the day knows his desperate need for the Spirit of God. He surrenders himself to the control of the Spirit, that God might work through him.

The man for the day has surrendered his future, his family, his time, his finances, and all of his resources to the Lord. He knows he owns nothing. He knows that he has earned nothing. He knows that he deserves nothing. Everything he has is a gift from God and belongs to God. He holds everything to God with an open hand.

The man for the day knows he is loved by God and, as a result, is not afraid to surrender fully to God. He rests in the confidence that what God has for him is always good. He knows God's plans are always best. He trusts God to write his story.

Be the man for the day!

Chapter 2

Preparation

Preparation: Letting God do the work in you that is necessary for the work God wants to do through you.

I ONCE HEARD someone pray a simple prayer that has been a part of my prayer life ever since. The prayer is, "Lord, do whatever You need to do in me so that You can do everything You want to do through me." That's a great prayer. It's a prayer God loves to hear, and a prayer God loves to answer.

It's a prayer of surrender. That's why, in some ways, it feels a little scary. "Lord, do whatever You need to do in me . . ." What a request! What an invitation! At times I'm not sure I really want the answer to that prayer. But, since surrender is the starting place for being the man for the day, and because perfect love casts out fear, we should joyfully ask the Lord to do whatever He needs to do in us. And as we pray it, we should rest in the loving heart of God who will only do what is best for us.

It's also a prayer of longing. That prayer is only prayed by someone who wants to be used by God. To pray that prayer is to say, "Lord, I want to be used by You no matter what the cost. I am ready and willing to experience anything You think I need for You to use me for Your purposes." In many ways, it's a prayer to be the man for the day.

It's also a prayer of preparation. It's a prayer that recognizes that for God to do something through me, He must first do something in me. There is a lot of wisdom in that prayer. God always works from the inside out. He begins a work in us before He does a work through us. For God to do something through you, He must first do something in you.

The words *need* and *want* are important in that little prayer. There is a work God *wants* to do, which is at the core of this book. But for that work to be done, there is a first work that God *needs* to do in us. There is a necessary work of preparation before there is the desired work of fulfillment. In order for God to work through us, He must first do a work in us. That is what we mean by preparation.

Preparation is letting God do the work in you that is necessary for the work God wants to do through you. Preparation is essential for being the man God is calling you to be. Every man who has ever been used of God can give many testimonies to preparation.

Some of this preparation is initiated by us. Some of this preparation is initiated by God. Sometimes the preparation is exhilarating. Sometimes the preparation is painful. Sometimes it makes sense, other times it feels like a mystery. But one thing is certain: For a man to be used by God, there must be long seasons of preparation. God is committed to this work. And we must be too.

Preparing Ourselves

In the fall of my senior year of high school, someone handed me a book titled *Hudson Taylor's Spiritual Secret.* Looking back and knowing how much I hated to read, I can't believe I ever read it. But I did, and it changed the trajectory of my life. It ignited a fire in my heart that I had never experienced before. Thirty years later, it is still the first book I recommend and give to high school and college students.

Hudson Taylor was a British Baptist missionary to China and the founder of the China Inland Mission. When every missionary to China stayed on the coast to reach the cities, Hudson Taylor took the gospel inland to the peoples who were the hardest to reach. He spent fifty-one years ministering in China, established twenty missionary outposts, recruited 849 missionaries, trained seven hundred native Chinese workers, and raised four million dollars (in the 1800s).[1]

However, the reason his book had such an impact on my life was not because of the effect of his ministry, but his own preparation for ministry. Once he had surrendered to the will of God for his life at the age of seventeen, he immediately began preparing for the work he believed God called him to. He knew his ministry in China would demand a tremendous amount of faith, so he began to prepare.

He moved to a poor suburb on the outskirts of town, began physical training, traded his feather bed for a hard cot, spent extended time with the Lord, and began working with the poorest people for barely enough money to survive. He had a vision of what he wanted God to do through him, so he began to prepare.[2] This was not the work of the flesh, but the movement of the Holy Spirit in his life.

In those early years, he wrote to his mother about this preparation:

> To me it was a very grave matter to contemplate going to China, far from all human aid, there to depend upon the living God alone for protection, supplies and help of every kind. I felt that one's spiritual muscles required strengthening for such an undertaking. There was no doubt that if faith did not fail, God would not fail. . . . When I get out to China I shall have no claim on anyone for anything. My only claim will be on God. How important to learn, before leaving England, to move man, through God, by prayer alone.[3]

Someone asked me recently why there is not more discipleship of men in the church. My answer was twofold: Pastors are not interested in a long-term approach to ministry, and most men aren't interested in a long-term approach to their life. Discipleship is a process. It's a process that bears more fruit ten years from now than it will ten days from now. The making of a godly man demands years of Spirit-fueled desire and discipline. It is not efficient. It is not immediate. But it is the way God builds men.

As Eugene Peterson said, "There is a great market for religious experience in our world; there is little enthusiasm for the patient acquisition of virtue. Little inclination to sign up for a long apprenticeship in what earlier generations called holiness."[4]

Jesus spent three years of ministry preparing twelve men for ministry. At the end of His ministry even His most beloved disciples deserted Him. Yet Jesus understood that men are *made*. They are developed over a long period of time through a lot of inner work of His Spirit.

If you are reading this book, I would imagine you have some desire to be the man God called you to be. As much as we want to see immediate results, the reality is, God does not usually work that way. He takes His time with us. Our outer activity is the result of the inner preparation of God's Spirit. If you want to be the man for the day, begin by doing the basic things consistently. Being God's man is less about doing any big things once and more about doing small things consistently. Read your Bible, commit to a local church, serve in that church, gather with a group of men for accountability, confess sin, give financially in a way that is sacrificial and consistent, make good use of your time, replace some entertainment for reading, and seek to live daily under the control of God's Spirit.

What does your current preparation indicate about your future effectiveness for the Lord? Are you preparing to be the man for the day? Are you being led by the Spirit of God?

Divine Preparation

Sometimes we prepare ourselves in the best way we know how. We do the right things repeatedly and watch God change us. But sovereign over all of that is God, who is committed to changing us and has promised to change us (Phil. 1:6). If Hudson Taylor taught me the need for personal preparation, Elijah taught me the need for divine preparation.

As we saw in the previous chapter, Elijah's ministry started off emphatically and dramatically. It seemed from the moment he appeared before King Ahab that his ministry was about to take off (1 Kings 17:1). But it didn't. At least not from a human perspective.

The next word Elijah received from God was, "Depart from here and turn eastward and hide yourself by the brook Cherith, which is east of the Jordan. You shall drink from the brook, and I have commanded the ravens to feed you there" (vv. 3–4 ESV).

That's not exactly the turn we expected his ministry to take—from speaking to the king to hiding for three years. That's right: It would be three years before Elijah would speak publicly again. Three years of obscurity.

The next verse simply says, "So he went and did according to the word of the LORD. He went and lived by the brook Cherith that is east of the Jordan" (v. 5 ESV). That is surrender. He had already lost the battle of the wills. He had surrendered to the Lord and trusted that God had a plan for him. Even if it didn't make sense, he knew God was right.

This must have been difficult. A prophet doesn't hide, a prophet speaks. And when a prophet's ministry starts by speaking directly to the king, you expect something big next. His ministry was just getting started. But God's next call was for him to hide. This makes no sense to us.

This is why surrender must be first. Because the way in which God chooses to sovereignly prepare you will almost never make sense to you so you have to trust that it makes sense to God. And you have to be willing to walk with Him in that.

What Elijah could not have fully realized—but what we see because we can read his whole story—is that those years of obscurity were essential preparation. I don't know if Elijah ever prayed, "Lord, do whatever You need to do in me so that You can do everything You want to do through me," but the Lord was doing that. God knew what He wanted to do with Elijah, and He knew what it would take to prepare him.

If you go back and read through 1 Kings 17, you will see that God was teaching Elijah to listen, to wait, and to trust. All the things that would be essential for the work God had for him. God was doing the work in him that needed to be done.

The reality is, the seasons of suffering, struggle, waiting, and searching are essential parts of God's preparation. And instead of rushing through them or resenting them, we must receive them as the good plan of God to prepare us for the work He wants to do through us.

God is doing that with you. We have a role in the change God wants to see and the preparation that needs to be done. But God is also working, by His Spirit, in ways we cannot see or cannot understand, yet in ways essential for what He knows is coming.

Trust the good, sovereign, loving plan of God as He is working in you and on you. The work may seem strange and will often feel difficult, but it's necessary.

Painful Preparation

One evening, right after Andrea had finished cancer treatment, we had some close friends over for dinner. They were talking to us about all we had been through, and I said, "It's been hard, but we wouldn't trade it for anything. We would do it all over again." To which Andrea quickly responded, "Sure, but next time you're getting cancer." We all laughed. I mean, easy for me to say. I'm not the one who almost died.

But it's true: We wouldn't trade that experience. Ten years later and we can still see the ways in which God used that to change us deeply. I can honestly say that I had never truly known the love of God until we went through that experience. But at the time, it certainly didn't feel that way.

Hudson Taylor experienced immense suffering while in China. He was a doctor and used those skills to travel around the country, meeting people's physical needs. Medical equipment was extremely difficult to get so he established a place to store them while he traveled. One day, upon returning home, he discovered that the storehouse had burned down and he had lost everything.

As much as he wanted to think that God was against him, he was reminded of Romans 8:28 and the truth that God is not only for him, but God is in all these hard things. Thinking about this moment he reflected, "I had not yet learned that *all* circumstances are necessarily the kindest, wisest, best, because either ordered or permitted by God."[5]

We all know what it's like to feel as though God is against us, especially when the painful experiences come. But we must rest in the good, gracious, kind, and perfect sovereignty of God and know that all these things are God's way of preparing us for what He wants to do through us.

Overwhelming Preparation

I have found so much encouragement over the years from the story of Jesus feeding the five thousand as recorded in John 6. The ultimate point of that story is that Jesus is the Bread of Life. But on another level, this story is about Jesus teaching something to the disciples.

Jesus sees the crowd and knows they need something to eat. He then turns to Philip and says, "Where are we to buy bread, so that these people may eat?" (v. 5 ESV). It's such a strange question because it's such a human impossibility. Andrew finds one kid with a small lunch, but there is no human way it can feed that many people.

The best part of the story is when it says, "He said this to test him, for he himself knew what he would do" (v. 6 ESV). In other words, before Jesus asked Philip about feeding the people, and before Andrew tried to steal a kid's lunch, Jesus already knew what He was going to do. So, why even bother the disciples? It was a test.

Jesus intentionally put His disciples in an overwhelming situation to test them; specifically, to test their faith. Why would He do this? Because Jesus knew the way in which He was going to use them after He was gone. He knew what He was going to do through them. But for Jesus to do that work through them, He must first do a work in them. And this is exactly what He was doing.

The principle is this: Our overwhelming situations are always God's gracious preparation. And not just the big ones. Not just the burned-down houses and cancer diagnoses. Every overwhelming situation in our lives, no matter how big or how small, is a part of God's gracious preparation.

The one who began a good work in us has promised to complete it (Phil. 1:6). He is navigating every circumstance and situation in our life to prepare us. Sometimes that preparation looks like Hudson Taylor's. The Spirit of God stirs up in us a strong desire to discipline ourselves for the purpose of godliness (1 Tim. 4:7–8). Sometimes, like Elijah, it looks like years of what feels like pointless waiting.

Sometimes the preparation is wonderful. Sometimes the preparation is painful. But one thing is for sure: We must trust God to do in us what He needs to do in order to do through us what He wants to do. God must prepare us to be the man for the day.

The Winding Road of Preparation

One of the great benefits of reading a story like Elijah's is being able to read his entire story in just a few moments. In a sense, we can see Elijah's life like God sees ours. We see the purpose behind all the things that seemed so confusing at the moment for Elijah. We can turn the page and see how God used his three years of hiding to prepare him. But when we stop and think about Elijah, we realize how hard those three years must have been. Three years is a long time to wait for God to tell you what's next.

But this is how God works. He sees life as a whole. He sees the start and the finish. He knows right now all the things He wants to accomplish through you. He knows the plans and purposes for your life (Jer. 29:11). And in His perfect sovereignty, God is mapping out the course of your life with perfect love and perfect wisdom to fulfill the purposes He has for you.

You just have to trust Him. You have to trust that every circumstance is a part of God's good preparation to make you the man for the day.

I love the way John Piper explains this often difficult journey of preparation:

> Life is not a straight line leading from one blessing to the next and then finally to heaven. Life is a winding and troubled road. Switchback after switchback. And the point of biblical stories like Joseph and Job and Esther and Ruth is to help us feel in our bones (not just know in our heads) that

> God is for us in all these strange turns. God is not just showing up after the trouble and cleaning it up. He is plotting the course and managing the troubles with far-reaching purposes for our good and for the glory of Jesus Christ.[6]

As you discipline yourself for godliness and trust God's sovereign plans for your life, you join God in doing the work in you that is necessary for the work He wants to do through you.

The Man for the Day

The man for the day knows that God works from the inside out. He knows that in order for God to do something through us, He must first do something in us.

The man for the day follows the leadership of the Holy Spirit when He prompts him to discipline himself for the purpose of godliness. He makes sacrifices in order to become the man God wants him to be.

The man for the day trusts the hard things of life as God's necessary preparation. Instead of resenting or ignoring the difficult seasons of life, he willingly embraces them as a gift from a loving and sovereign God.

The man for the day welcomes the work of God's Spirit in molding him and making him a useful man.

Be the man for the day!

Chapter 3

Direction

Direction: Seeing every moment as a significant step in becoming the man God wants you to be.

MY FATHER SPENT the last thirty-five years of his life as a traveling evangelist. He had spent the previous twenty-five years serving as a local church pastor. But even as a pastor, he was an evangelist; his heart always beat for the lost. It wasn't just a passion, it was a gifting from God (Eph. 4:11–12). When he preached, people were saved.

Every church my father pastored saw explosive growth. Every Sunday people would give their lives to Christ and be baptized. Then, when he transitioned to being a full-time traveling evangelist, everywhere he went, small towns or big towns, small churches or football stadiums, people were saved.

This is what I grew up seeing. What a blessing! In my mind, this kind of response to the gospel was normal. Seeing twenty people baptized at church was just another Sunday. Seeing a hundred people saved in a stadium was just another Tuesday night. I assumed this is how it always happened.

When I became a pastor, it didn't take long for me to realize that what I had grown up seeing actually wasn't normal. What I saw every week is something that most people never see and something that I would rarely see in my own ministry. It took me years not only to understand the nature of God's gifting, but even more so to understand the way God normally works.

I grew up assuming that God's work was always big work. Always dramatic. Always life-changing. Always bigger than the last. As a result, I didn't make time for the small work. I wanted big work, and anything less than that seemed like a waste of time.

That idea not only affected my ministry but my own spiritual progress. But as I have learned, if you only view God's work as big work, you will miss most of the work God intends to do.

Our lives will include some dramatic moments, even some seasons of dramatic spiritual progress. If we walk faithfully with the Lord, we will have seasons that feel like we are running at full speed and can never be stopped. But we *will* stop. That pace cannot be sustained forever.

At some point, we will realize the truth: God's work is usually slow and small work, not just His work through us, but His work in us. He works through the little moments. He changes us through the small things. He prepares us to be the men He has called us to be not through a spiritual boot camp but through the normal course of our often mundane lives. Day by day, step-by-step, moment by moment, God is changing us.

Direction Over Distance

A turning point in my understanding of how God normally works in our lives—the way God makes us into the men we are called to be—came in the form of one simple idea: When it comes to our spiritual lives, direction matters more than distance. The most important factor in our spiritual progress is not how fast we are going but that we are moving in the right direction. The world is filled with men running fast—in the wrong direction. It looks like progress, but it's not. It's just heading toward the wrong destination faster.

This idea of direction over distance was embedded into my heart through the writings of David Powlison. This illustration of his is helpful:

> Do you remember any high school math? "A man drives the 300 miles from Boston to Philadelphia. He goes 60 mph for 2 hours and 40 mph for 3 hours, then sits in traffic for 1 hour not moving. If traffic lightens up and he can drive the rest of the way at 30 mph, how many hours will the whole trip take?" If you know the formula "distance equals rate times time," you can figure it out (8 hours!). Is sanctification like that, a calculation of how far and how fast for how long?

> Not really. The key question in sanctification is whether you're even heading in the direction of Philadelphia. If you're heading west toward Seattle, you can drive 75 mph for as long as you want, but you'll never, ever get to Philadelphia. And if you're simply sitting outside Boston and have no idea which direction you're supposed to go, you'll never get anywhere. But if you're heading in the right direction, you can go 10 mph or 60 mph. You can get stuck in traffic and sit awhile. You can get out and walk. You can crawl on your hands and knees. You can even get temporarily turned around and head the wrong way for a while. But you get straightened out again. At some point you'll get where you need to go.[1]

As much as I wish life was filled with dramatic moments and seasons in which we feel like we are driving full speed ahead toward Jesus, the reality is, most of life feels like we are crawling on our hands and knees. But as Powlison reminds us, crawling on our hands and knees toward Jesus is better than sprinting toward anything else.

If we don't believe that deeply in our souls, we will miss most of the work God is trying to do in our lives. We will sacrifice direction for distance and just end up getting to the wrong place faster.

Following God's Word

Elijah stood before King Ahab and declared that it would not rain until he said so. That's how his ministry started—one big, dramatic moment. Then, in order for the Lord to prepare him, the Lord led him to a secluded place and made him hide in obscurity for three years. The Lord knew what was ahead and was graciously preparing Elijah for it. To Elijah, however, it must have seemed like wasted time. But no moment is wasted in the providence of God.

One of the secrets to Elijah being the man for the day was his willingness to just keep moving. He just kept doing the next right thing. He heard from the Lord and did what the Lord told him to do. One step at a time. Elijah trusted that the direction of his life mattered more than distance. If he didn't, he would have never been the man God called him to be. This is how God prepared him, and this is how God prepares us. We see this over and over in 1 Kings 17.

Immediately after Elijah took the step of obedience to speak to King Ahab it says, "And the word of the LORD came to him: 'Depart from here and turn eastward and hide yourself by the brook Cherith, which is east of the Jordan. You shall drink from the brook, and I have commanded the ravens to feed you there'" (vv. 2–4 ESV). Nothing about this made sense. This was not a command of distance. This was a command of direction.

What would Elijah do? "So he went and did according to the word of the LORD. He went and lived by the brook Cherith that is east of the Jordan. And the ravens brought him bread and meat in the morning, and bread and meat in the evening, and he drank from the brook. And after a while the brook dried up, because there was no rain in the land" (vv. 5–7 ESV).

He obeyed. He took the next step. He moved in the right direction. And instead of that leading to a life of immediate overflowing abundance, it led to a dried-up creek. What would he do next?

"Then the word of the LORD came to him, 'Arise, go to Zarephath, which belongs to Sidon, and dwell there. Behold, I have commanded a widow there to feed you'" (vv. 8–9 ESV). And then it says, "So he arose and went to Zarephath . . ." (v. 10 ESV).

Elijah took the next step in the right direction. And this was Elijah's life for three years. For three years Elijah took one step of obedience at a time. If Elijah had been consumed with distance, he would not have been able to simply move in the direction of obedience. And if he had not learned to simply move in that direction, he would have never been prepared for what God had for him in the future.

After three years of obscure preparation, God led Elijah into something that finally felt like distance. "After many days the word of the LORD came to Elijah, in the third year, saying, 'Go, show yourself to Ahab, and I will send rain upon the earth.' So, Elijah went to show himself to Ahab" (18:1–2a ESV).

In those years of preparation, we see a pattern emerge. A pattern that would determine both the direction and distance of Elijah's life. The pattern is: The Lord spoke, and Elijah obeyed. That is one of the most important secrets to Elijah's life. Elijah learned to walk in the direction of obedience even when that direction did not seem to lead to distance.

Obedience to the Lord, in the smallest things of life, is always the right direction, and always the pathway toward greater distance. Every step Elijah took in the right direction, God met him there, God used him, and God prepared him for what was next. All of that would have been missed if he had not simply kept moving in the right direction. This was the pattern of Elijah's life. And it must be the pattern of ours as well.

The Most Important Step

In the midst of all the seemingly mundane steps of obedience, Elijah experienced some pretty dramatic things along the way. It was in Cherith that he sat by the brook during a severe famine and was supernaturally fed by ravens every morning and every evening.

It was in Zarephath where he met a widow who was about to cook her last meal and prepare for her and her son to die of starvation. But Elijah told her to cook some bread with her last handful of flour and the little oil she had. He promised her that if she did this, her flour and oil would never run out. And it never did.

It was also in Zarephath when the widow's son died and she was overcome with grief and anger at Elijah. But Elijah cried out to the Lord, stretched himself upon the child three times, and begged the Lord to raise him. And the Lord did; the boy was raised to life.

It was that third step of obedience that ultimately led Elijah to his greatest moment when he went to battle with the prophets of Baal on Mount Carmel. That would be the defining moment of Elijah's life.

The only way he got to those dramatic moments is by walking in obedience even in the seemingly mundane moments. Every one of Elijah's greatest moments happened along the pathway of obedience. Even when that pathway of obedience did not look like it was heading any place significant, it always was.

The reason I continually use the words "seemingly mundane moments" is because that's what most of life feels like to us. But that is not the way God sees us. The seemingly mundane moments are the moments God is making you into the man he wants you to be. Obedience to the promptings and conviction of the Holy Spirit is the way in which God makes godly men.

This is the lesson that begins to emerge from the life of Elijah. It is one of the most important lessons we will ever learn. It is in many ways the key to fulfilling every work God has for us. It is at the very core of being prepared and willing to be the man for the day.

The principle of direction is this: Every moment is a significant step in making you into the man God wants you to be. The most important step you take is the next one, so make sure it's a step in the right direction.

Read through the list of all the men used of God through the Bible, and you will see this to be true. Think about Abraham. Abraham was the man for the day. God came to him in Genesis 12 and gave him an incredible vision of his future, an almost unbelievable vision that He would make him into a great nation, bless him, and make his name great. Through Abraham, God said, all the families of the earth will be blessed (v. 3b). That's an incredible vision of the future!

The question is: How will Abraham get there? How will he fulfill all that God has for him? The answer is found in Hebrews 11:8: "By faith Abraham obeyed when he was called to go out to a place that he was to receive as an inheritance. And he went out, not knowing where he was going" (ESV).

In order for Abraham to fulfill all God had for him, he had to start walking in that direction. Having no idea where he was going or where it was leading, he trusted that the most important step was the next one, and he walked in the right direction. The way God fulfilled His big vision for Abraham was in Abraham taking small steps of faith.

Every step we take is moving us in a direction. We can either mindlessly move in the wrong direction or mindfully move in the right direction. But know this: Every step matters. No step is insignificant. Do you see how this changes your view of becoming the man God wants you to be? It means that the way to get there is always by small steps. Every day, moving in the direction you want to go.

Not only are those steps moving you toward where you want to go, those steps are making you into the man God wants you to be in the process. It is in those steps that God prepares us, forms us, molds us, and uses us. Every step is about progress. Every step is about you surrendering to the way God builds men—one step at a time.

Being the Man Today

Let's go back to what Spurgeon said: "Here is the day for the man, where is the man for the day?"[2] We want to be the man for the day—the man who is ready and willing to do whatever God calls him to do. My prayer is that idea would stir up longing and desire in your heart. The man for the day is the greatest need of every generation.

But as we see the way in which God worked through Elijah, preparing him to be the man for the day, one thing is clear: Becoming the man for the day is about being that man today.

What matters most in your spiritual progress and preparation is today. If this is true, the practical implications for us are huge. Every moment matters. Not just because every moment is about preparation, but because every moment is about progress.

When I speak to men, I not only like to lay a foundation for godly manhood, I like to give a lot of practical advice that will help move them in the right direction. I want them to go home with some things that will help them today.

I encourage men to go to work and work hard and then come home and work hard. Come home and be engaged, helpful, and active with your wife and kids.

I encourage men to go home and not be grumpy. It sounds silly, but I believe one of the greatest things a man can do to dramatically change his home life is to come home from work with a happy, joyful, encouraging, and affirming spirit. This is no small challenge, but one I think about in my own life all the time.

I tell men that it's impossible to say you are committed to Jesus if you are not committed to his bride, the church. You cannot say Jesus has priority in your life if the church does not have priority in your life. I call men to serve faithfully, give consistently and sacrificially, and make the bride of Christ a priority in their home.

I challenge men to make a commitment to spend time with God every single day. Not giving God any leftover time you have, but giving Him your best time. The truth is that the one thing that is most needed to build a relationship with Jesus is the one thing we least like to give Jesus: time!

I challenge men to wage absolute war on sexual sin. Not just in the external practices, but in the battleground of the mind. I plead with men to get honest about their struggles and immediately and aggressively seek the help they need.

I give all of these practical challenges because I want to reiterate that becoming the man for the day is about being that man today. Those little decisions to go home and work hard, go home with a good attitude, give, serve, spend time with God, and fight sin, are all steps in the right direction. And over time, those little steps in the right direction will make you God's man in the process.

Men, today is about preparation and progress. Direction means walking with Jesus today. It means saying no to sin today. Don't worry about saying no to sin forever. Just say no to sin right now.

This moment matters as much as any other. This moment is *the* moment. This is the moment that will determine your direction.

When You Stop Moving

Let me give you one final warning. Talking about the generation of Israelites who wandered through the wilderness and ultimately missed the blessings of God, the book of Hebrews warns us to persevere and keep moving in the right direction. Each step is a step of faith.

Among all of the warnings in Hebrews, the one in Hebrews 2:1 is particularly helpful for us here. It says, "We must pay much closer attention to what we have heard, lest we drift away from it" (ESV).

At times, we willfully choose to move in the wrong direction. We know what is right, and we don't do it. We make choices to sin, taking steps away from the life God has for us. Every time we do that, we sow to the flesh and reap corruption instead of sowing to the Spirit and reaping life (Gal. 6:8). In other words, every step away from Jesus is a step away from the life that Jesus wants to give us.

And we all do it. We sin. We choose to walk away from Jesus and move in the wrong direction. Every one of those steps matter. They hinder our progress, steal our joy, and keep us from being the men God has called us to be.

The warning of Hebrews 2 is not as much about willful disobedience as it is about thoughtless wandering. We just don't think about our direction at all. We just live. We just exist. We just make it through another day.

Proverbs 4:26 commands us to "ponder the path of [our] feet" (ESV). Ephesians 5:15 commands us to be careful how we walk. Our steps matter. Our moments matter. And unless we are making intentional steps in the right direction, we will be drifting in the wrong direction. We never stay still; we are always headed somewhere. We are headed toward Jesus, or away from Him. But we never just stand still.

So to become the men God wants us to be, we must continually make the moment by moment choices to head in the direction of Jesus—eyes on Him, filled with His Spirit, small steps of obedience, step-by-step, always moving; not worrying about distance, just worrying about direction. If you want to be useful to God someday, be obedient to God today.

Just Keep Moving

My dearest friend in the world has been going through a season of what seems like unrelenting suffering. Walking through this with him has been one of the hardest seasons of my life. And I'm not even the one suffering.

Over the past few months we have talked multiple times a week, often multiple times a day. Every time we talk, I just pray that the Lord will give me something to encourage him. Recently, that has been getting more and more difficult.

This friend tends to be very optimistic. He almost always follows some statement of incredible suffering with something like, "But honestly, I think this is going to turn out great." To which I want to respond, "I don't see any way this is going to turn out great."

But recently, for the very first time, I began to hear a bit of unusual uncertainty in his voice. It was more than a hint of discouragement; it was the sound of emerging despondency. As I listened to him talk, I just began to pray, as always, that the Lord would give me some word to encourage him. I didn't have anything. I just listened. I hung up. I prayed.

Over the next few days, I asked the Lord to give me a word for him. And He did. But it wasn't much, nor was it all that profound. I felt like it was from the Lord. I prayed again. I picked up the phone and I called him. He answered, and all I said was, "God is not done with you. Keep moving."

It's the principle of direction: The most important step we take is the next one, so make sure it's a step in the right direction.

I wish it was more profound. I wish it felt more spectacular. I wish it bore more immediate fruit and showed more immediate results. But in reality, it's the secret to becoming the man God created you to be. We just believe that God's not done. We keep moving. We keep moving in the right direction.

Most of life comes down to this: Keep moving. And keep moving in the right direction. Direction always matters more than distance. If you take care of the direction, God will take care of the distance. We just keep walking. Every moment matters. Because God is working in you, and every small and insignificant moment is the process. Every one of those moments is making you into the man He wants you to be. If you want to be the man for the day, you must be that man today.

The Man for the Day

The man for the day thinks about today. He sees every moment as significant. He knows that to be useful to God someday, he must be obedient to God today.

The man for the day sees every mundane moment as a significant moment. He chooses to walk with God and do the right thing throughout the day because he knows that's the way God builds men.

The man for the day is serious about the small things. He trusts the Lord will do the big work if he commits to do the small work.

Be the man for the day!

Chapter 4

Courage

Courage: The spiritual strength to do and say what is right no matter the cost or consequences.

THERE ONCE LIVED a man who was a coward. He was always scared and ran away from everything he feared. He had been a coward his entire life. Tired of living that way, he went to a wise man for guidance and asked if the man could teach him how to be brave.

The wise man agreed to help him and gave him one simple assignment. The wise man told him, "For one month, you must say to every person you meet and everyone who crosses your path, 'I am a coward,' and you must say it loudly while looking straight into their eyes."

The man was now even more terrified. He could not bear the thought of so many humiliating encounters. For the first few days he stood motionless at the sight of everyone who passed by. But he knew that if he was ever going to learn to be brave, he must finish this difficult task. So, on the third day, he mustered up all the courage he had, saw a man passing by, looked him directly in the eye, and softly said, "I am a coward."

In a moment, after that first encounter, something began to change. With every other person who passed by, his voice became louder and more confident. In a few days, he was no longer scared and could approach anyone with the simple words the wise man told him to say.

After a few weeks he went to thank the wise man. He joyfully reported that after finishing the task, he was no longer afraid. In so doing, he realized what the wise man already knew—sometimes a man can only find his courage by openly acknowledging he is a coward.[1]

Bold as a Lion

I've always wanted to live up to my namesake, Joshua. He was called to lead the people into the promised land. As he was preparing to do so, the resounding message from the Lord was simple: "Be strong and courageous" (Josh. 1:6). And he was.

Joshua was the man for the day. His life was marked by strength and courage. There has always been something deep inside of me that longs to be that kind of man. I want to be strong. I want to be courageous. I imagine you do too.

Maybe this is why I love lions. If you walked into my office, it would be obvious how much I love lions. You wouldn't find real lions or massive stone statues of lions (and this is only because it's illegal to have a real one and my wife thinks massive stone ones are tacky), but you would find paintings, pictures, and many wood carvings of them. One of the reasons I love lions is because my favorite verse is Proverbs 28:1, which says, "The wicked flee when no one is pursuing them, but the righteous are as bold as a lion." What a verse! The righteous are bold like a lion. I love that!

Revelation 21:8 contains one of those lists of all the people who will not enter into the kingdom of God. It tells us that the faithless, the detestable, the murderers, the sexually immoral, sorcerers, idolaters, and all the liars will spend eternity in the lake that burns with fire.

Although this list in Revelation looks like just another list of vices frequently used in the New Testament or even one of the three already used in Revelation, this list is different. This list highlights the specific sins of the book of Revelation as a whole. This is why this list does not start with the faithless or idolaters. It doesn't even start with the murderers or sorcerers. This list begins with the cowards. "But the cowards . . . will be in the lake that burns with fire . . ."

Cowardice is first on the list because the coward is contrasted with the "one who conquers" and gains eternal life in the previous verse (v. 7). The reason the mention of the coward is here right after the overcomer is because "the reader is being asked to choose whether to 'overcome' the pressures of the world and refuse to succumb to it or to be a 'coward' and surrender to sin."[2] According to Revelation 21, the choice between cowardice and courage is the choice between heaven and hell.

This is why Proverbs 28:1 says that "the righteous are as bold as a lion." The calling to follow Jesus Christ, and certainly the calling to be the man for the day, demands we have a heart full of courage. Courage is not an option. Cowardice is not a choice. Men of God are courageous. Cowards are listed among the sorcerers and idolaters. It would certainly seem that to be the man for the day, courage is mandatory and cowardice is not an option. That's true. But maybe, in some ways, it's not that simple.

Obadiah: Courage . . . and Cowardice

While Elijah was in his season of obscure preparation, King Ahab was trying to find him. The last time he saw Elijah was when Elijah declared that it would not rain until he said so. Although this was the judgment of God on the wickedness of Ahab, Ahab was convinced this famine was Elijah's fault. This means instead of repenting of his wickedness and turning back to God, Ahab focused on finding Elijah and telling him to make it rain.

While King Ahab was trying to find Elijah, his wife, Queen Jezebel, was systematically finding every prophet of Yahweh and killing them. There is a reason the name Jezebel is associated with evil. It's hard to find someone more evil than Queen Jezebel. Her great ambition during her reign was to ensure every prophet of Yahweh and place of worship of Yahweh was destroyed and replaced with the worship of the god Baal and the goddess Asherah. And as we learn from her story, when she wanted something, she got it.

It is in that moment, when Elijah was in a season of obscurity, King Ahab was hunting for Elijah, and Queen Jezebel was hunting down prophets, that a man by the name of Obadiah emerged. He was King Ahab's chief of staff (1 Kings 18:3a). He was the head of Ahab's household, which means he was powerful, influential, and trusted by the king.

But Obadiah had secrets, most significantly, the secret that he loved God. We are told that he "feared the LORD greatly" (v. 3b ESV) and the evidence of that is seen in what he did. "When Jezebel cut off the prophets of the LORD, Obadiah took a hundred prophets and hid them by fifties in a cave and fed them with bread and water" (v. 4 ESV).

Think about that. Imagine the amount of courage it would take to do that. The king's most trusted advisor was hiding the prophets that his wife, Queen Jezebel, was trying to kill. Amazing!

It doesn't take long, though, to realize that Obadiah is a mystery. We know he loved the Lord and was willing to do the hard things the Lord asked him to do, yet still, he was the chief of staff for the most wicked king God's people had ever seen. He had a front-row seat to the slaughtering of God's prophets. Every day he worked alongside the one on whom the judgment of God rested. And, although courageous in some ways, he was terrified in others.

The next time we hear from Elijah, he is meeting with Obadiah and telling him to go tell King Ahab that he is ready to meet. Obadiah responds: "How have I sinned, that you would give your servant into the hand of Ahab, to kill me? As the LORD your God lives, there is no nation or kingdom where my lord has not sent to seek you" (vv. 9–10a ESV). To which Elijah responds again: "Go, tell your lord, 'Behold, Elijah is here'" (v.11 ESV). This little song and dance goes on for a while. But finally, after much debate, Obadiah goes.

The man who dared to risk his life to hide the prophets of God and keep them fed was terrified of approaching Ahab on behalf of Elijah. History has struggled to know exactly what to do with Obadiah. We honor him because he hid the prophets, but we are baffled by the depth of his fear. We honor him because he feared the Lord, but we question his close association with such an evil king.

It's difficult to know what to do with Obadiah because he does not fit neatly as either a hero or villain. We like our heroes heroic and our villains villainous. But there is only one perfect hero in the Bible, and Obadiah is certainly not a villain. So, what is he? We don't have a category for him. And although we find ourselves puzzled by the mystery of this seemingly complicated man, maybe he's here to be a picture of us. A profile of courage . . . and cowardice.

Elijah: Courage . . . and Cowardice

Although there are many helpful definitions of courage, it seems that courage is better demonstrated than defined. And we will not get a better demonstration than by what Elijah did next.

When Obadiah finally told Ahab that Elijah wanted to see him, the two met face-to-face.

"When Ahab saw Elijah, Ahab said to him, 'Is that you, the one ruining Israel?' He replied, 'I have not ruined Israel, but you and your father's family have, because you have abandoned the Lord's commands and followed the Baals'" (vv. 17–18).

For three years Ahab had been trying to find Elijah because he believed the famine was Elijah's fault since Elijah was the one who said it would not rain again until he said so. But when Ahab tried to blame Elijah for this, Elijah made it clear that this was no one's fault but Ahab's. Ahab was the one ruining Israel. This famine was the judgment of God for Ahab's evil.

In the rest of 1 Kings 18, Elijah gives us what might be the greatest demonstration of courage in the entire Old Testament (events we will look at in more detail later). Elijah summoned all the false prophets—450 of Baal and 400 of Asherah—to Mount Carmel, and challenged the 450 prophets of Baal to prove who was God.

They set up two altars, one for Baal and one for Yahweh. The challenge: The god who answers by fire is the real, more powerful, god.

The 450 prophets of Baal went first. They prayed, they danced, they marched, they cut themselves. All while Elijah watched and mocked them. Their god did nothing.

When it was Elijah's turn, he prayed, calling on God to make Himself known, and watched as the fire came from heaven and consumed the altar. As if that wasn't victory enough, Elijah then led the prophets of Baal to the brook Kishon, where he slaughtered them all! That's courage!

Elijah then told Ahab it was about to rain when there was no cloud in the sky. Elijah got on his knees and prayed until there was a cloud the size of his hand. He got up and outran Ahab's chariot on foot! This guy was incredible! He was unstoppable.

Then, the most surprising thing happened. Right after this incredible display of strength and courage, Elijah got word that Jezebel wanted to kill him. But who cares, right? This is Elijah! He just slaughtered 450 false prophets!

Surprisingly, Elijah was terrified. He ran deep into the woods; sat all alone, wallowing in self-pity; and prayed that God would take his life.

We didn't see that coming. But there it is. Elijah, a man of deep courage . . . and, at times, deep cowardice.

A Little Courage . . . a Little Cowardice

Maybe it's because I've always loved my namesake, Joshua, or because of my love for lions. Maybe it's because I've had some defining moments in my life that have formed this idea, or it's just delusion or wishful thinking. I don't know exactly why it is, but for some reason, I have always thought of myself as courageous. That is, until recently.

What I have discovered, in a deeply troubling way, is that I am both courageous and cowardly. I'm Obadiah. I'm Elijah. Not so much in their courage, but in their cowardice.

There are areas in my life in which I have demonstrated courage. I have made hard decisions, done hard things, had hard conversations, and stood for what was right when no one else did. I have done and said the right things no matter the cost. I have had moments of courage.

And yet, in the midst of all that, I have become increasingly aware of how many hard things I avoid. More and more, I am noticing how many things I neglect to do even though I know they are right. I am seeing more and more conversations that I am refusing to have and decisions I am failing to make, even though I know I should. The moments of courage are often overshadowed by the moments of cowardice.

More and more, the Lord is showing me the ways in which I fail to be courageous. And more and more, the Lord is showing me this in the men I minister to.

It is possible for a man to be courageous on the battlefield and be a coward at home. He might stand face-to-face with an enemy, but not face-to-face with his wife. He might be willing to exhaust himself near the point of death for the sake of his country, but come home and barely raise a finger to engage with his wife and kids.

A man might be a fierce protector of his family's physical life, but a coward when it comes to protecting them from social, moral, cultural, and sexual enemies that are attacking them every day.

A man might courageously say, "As for me and my house, we will serve the LORD" (Josh. 24:15b ESV), but will not have the courage to say no to the countless activities that take him and his family away from church.

A man might have the necessary and difficult conversation with an employee, but will not have the necessary and difficult conversation with a friend. He might never avoid a conversation that would affect the bottom line at work, but will harbor bitterness and resentment for years instead of having a hard conversation at home.

A man might stand courageously between his daughter and someone trying to assault her, but will not stand between his daughter and her phone. Yet the chances of his daughter getting assaulted by a stranger are much less likely than her being morally, emotionally, and spiritually harmed by what she sees on her device.

A man might jokingly bring a shotgun to the door when a young man comes to pick up his daughter for a date, but will not take the time to communicate his expectations and boundaries before he leaves the house with his daughter. Taking a shotgun to the door is not a bad move, but it will never take the place of having difficult conversations with his daughter about the kind of man she can date. Or even more so, having a difficult conversation with every man who wants to take his daughter out.

There are men who will loudly declare their political convictions when no one wants to hear them, but will not open their mouths to share the gospel when there is a wide-open door.

Many men can make some strong and passionate statements about politicians and their political positions, but never demonstrate the same strength and passion when talking about Jesus.

How many men are there who can go on a twenty-minute rant against the evils of the nation, but fail to talk to their children about the movies they are watching and the music they are listening to?

And what about the man who bemoans the moral decline of our nation, but does not wage war against his own moral sin? He is courageous when speaking about the perversity of others, but a coward when dealing with the perversity in his own heart and mind.

If we are honest with ourselves, we must acknowledge that we might not be as courageous as we think we are. There is some courage and cowardice in all of us. The only way we move on to more courage and less cowardice is by acknowledging all the ways and all the areas in which we lack it.

The Battle for Courage

Although it can be discouraging to see the cowardice in ourselves, it shouldn't be surprising. This is the story of the Bible. Abraham, who displayed great courage in trusting the Lord to leave his home, continued to lie about his wife because he didn't trust God to protect her. David, who killed Goliath, later slept with another man's wife and killed the woman's husband instead of acknowledging his guilt. Simon Peter, who cut off a soldier's ear in the garden, denied Jesus when asked by a young girl if he was a disciple. The battle between courage and cowardice rages in all of us.

Why is this the case? Why will every man battle between courage and cowardice? Why will we all tend to be courageous in some areas and cowards in others?

It's because a battle between courage and cowardice is really just a battle between the Spirit and the flesh. When walking in the Spirit, we have courage. When walking in the flesh, we are cowards.

This is Paul's point in Romans 7:14–25. There is a very real battle waging inside our souls every moment of the day. And so many times, even when we long to be courageous, when the moment arises, we become cowards. We don't do what we want to do or say what needs to be said. Our good intentions turn into failed attempts. And once again, we stand frustrated and angry over our ability to do and say the right thing.

This is the reason we have defined courage the way we have. Courage is *the spiritual strength to do and say what is right no matter the cost or consequences.* The first three words of that definition are the most important.

Courage is a matter of spiritual strength. We are not looking for courage that we muster up by an act of the will, but courage that is a real manifestation of the power of the Spirit of God in us. It is a courage that increases as we choose, day by day, moment by moment, to walk in the Spirit and not in the flesh.

When we choose to sow to the Spirit, we will inherit life, which will manifest itself in courage. When we sow to the flesh, we will not only reap spiritual death but the manifestation of that spiritual death, which is cowardice (Gal. 6:8).

Elijah's unmatched courage in 1 Kings 18 is a manifestation of a man full of the Spirit of God. Elijah's deep cowardice in 1 Kings 19 is the manifestation of a man who is spiritually, physically, and emotionally depleted. Courage is weak when the Spirit is weak. Courage is strong when the Spirit is strong. As Paul told Timothy, "God has not given us a spirit of fear, but one of power, love, and sound judgment" (2 Tim. 1:7). The cowardly spirit is not from the Spirit of God.

Our primary battle is not against cowardice and for courage, but against the flesh and for the fullness of the Spirit. If you just fight for courage, you will not get courage or the Spirit. But if you fight for the fullness of the Spirit, you will get the Spirit and courage.

The primary reason most men lack courage for the things of God is because they are walking around morally defeated. If you are constantly being defeated by sin, then you will have no sense of courage. You will walk around feeling like you have already lost. That is why the battle for courage must ultimately be a battle for the Spirit. The first battlefield in which you need courage is the battlefield of your moral purity and your time alone with God. When you have the courage in those areas, the Spirit will give you the wisdom and courage needed for every other area.

It is also the Spirit that keeps our courage in check. It is the Spirit that ensures we are not only courageous, but courageous about the things that matter most. It is the Spirit who shows us that the courage we most often need is the courage we most often neglect. The Spirit not only empowers us with courage; He shows us how, where, and when to use it. We don't need men full of courage for the wrong things, but men full of courage for things that matter most.

To be the man for the day you must be ready and willing to say and do whatever is right, no matter the cost or consequences. That demands one thing above all: the Spirit of God.

Because in our flesh, we are all cowards, but the Spirit makes us courageous.

Courage Is *Not* an Option

If you have any desire to be the man for the day, this is a battle you must fight. You must fight against the temptation of the Enemy who wants you to be a coward like him. He hates spiritual courage. He disdains courageous men. Why? Because truly courageous men use their courage against the Enemy and his attacks. They will not sit still while the Enemy tries to win.

Courage is not an option for the man who wants to be used by God. There are many reasons for this. First, your calling demands it. Courage is the calling of godly manhood (1 Cor. 16:13). You cannot be a godly man without seeking courage by seeking the fullness of the Spirit. You cannot be the friend, husband, father, or church member God has called you to be without it. Every part of your calling demands courage.

Second, God's commission demands it. We must lead the way in taking the gospel to the unreached peoples. The reason they are unreached is because of how hard it is to get to them. We must lead the way in this. Sometimes, however, it seems that taking the gospel to the tribes in Nepal is easier than taking the gospel to the guy next door. When is the last time you shared the gospel with anyone? If it's been a while, it's most likely for the lack of courage.

Third, spiritual warfare demands it. There is an Enemy who wants to devour you and your family (1 Pet. 5:8). The Enemy is assaulting you and those you love. The reality of that constant warfare demands courage. You must take your stand against him.

Finally, our current culture demands it. The man for the day is a man who understands the times and is willing to stand for God in those times! There is no more time and no more room for men who call themselves Christians yet refuse to stand for the truth of Christ in our culture. Who is standing against the moral insanity of the culture in which we live? If we are to be the light and salt of the world (Matt. 5:13–16), we must have the courage to stand for what is right.

Say You're a Coward

It seems that God has placed in almost every man some measure of courage. At least He has placed in every man a desire for courage. Many nights I lay in bed thinking of how courageous I would be, play-by-play and in slow-motion, if an intruder came into my home. It's never been a reality, but I have to believe if that moment were to happen, there would be at least a small amount of courage.

We will not grow in true courage, the courage that comes from the Spirit, by reflecting on how courageous we are or imagining how courageous we could be. As strange as it seems, and as much as this goes against all positive self-talk, what we need the most to cultivate courage is the ability to say, like the man at the beginning of the chapter, "I am a coward," at least in so many things that matter, and I need God's help.

We should not only say it because it's true in so many areas of our lives, but we should also say it because honesty and humility are the breeding ground for a new work of God. That is always the starting ground for spiritual growth (James 4:6). If we want to be strong and courageous, we must first acknowledge that we are weak and cowardly. At least in some areas of our lives. And there, at that place of weakness, God will begin to work by the power of His Spirit, to make us into the man He wants us to be and we long to be.

C. S. Lewis observed in *The Screwtape Letters* that cowardice is the only vice in which no person is proud.[3] Nothing is worse for a boy than being called a chicken, and nothing is worse for a man than being called a coward. Everything in us recoils against cowardice. That's a good thing. We need that hatred for cowardice to drive us to our knees in humble admission of how much help we need to overcome it.

Let us, by God's grace, acknowledge that we don't want to be cowards. Let us hate cowardice with every ounce of our being. Allow that to move us toward becoming the men God has called us to be—men who have the spiritual strength to do and say what is right no matter the cost or consequences. That's what it takes to be the man for the day.

The Man for the Day

The man for the day knows that the work of God demands courage. He knows that everything, from fighting personal sin to standing against cultural insanity, demands courage.

The man for the day is honest about his areas of cowardice. He sees the areas in which he lacks courage and will honestly admit his need for help. He will humbly admit his need for courage to God and others so that he might see God change him.

The man for the day knows that courage comes from the Spirit of God. He does not fight for courage, but for more of God's Spirit. He knows the cowardly spirit is from the flesh and the courageous spirit is from God.

The man for the day does not just want to be courageous; he pursues courage by pursuing purity of heart and the fullness of the Spirit.

Be the man for the day!

Chapter 5

Resolve

Resolve: The firm determination to walk with God.

JONATHAN EDWARDS IS arguably the most influential preacher, pastor, theologian, and philosopher in American history. Although he is most known for his famous sermon, "Sinners in the Hands of an Angry God," his key role in America's first Great Awakening and his impact on world missions are unmatched. Remarkably, the impact of his life in his generation is only exceeded by the impact of his life on future generations. He was a giant of the faith.

Anyone who reads his works will be quickly amazed by his intellect. He had a brilliant mind and an unbelievable breadth of knowledge. But what made him unique was that his brilliant mind was combined with a remarkable ability to preach and practically apply God's Word.

However, those who have studied his life carefully would say that none of those gifts and skills were the secret to his greatness. The secret to the life of this spiritual giant was his "resolve."

When Edwards was eighteen years old, just a year after his conversion, while serving as the associate pastor of a church in New York City, he began to write what he called his "Resolutions." In approximately one year, he wrote seventy resolutions for his life.

These resolutions became a sort of mission statement for his life that would guide him in his path and pursuit of godliness. He was a man determined to walk with God, and those resolutions would be the practical outworking of that firm determination.

A list of resolutions was not a new idea to Edwards. It would be equivalent to us making New Year's resolutions, if New Year's resolutions were thought of in terms of resolutions for one's entire life and if they were not forgotten by March.

He began his resolutions with these words: "Being sensible that I am unable to do any thing without God's help, I do humbly entreat him, by his grace, to enable me to keep these Resolutions, so far as they are agreeable to his will, for Christ's sake. *Remember to read over these Resolutions once a week.*"[1]

Here are a few of his seventy resolutions:

- *Resolved,* That I will do whatsoever I think to be most to the glory of God, and my own good, profit, and pleasure, in the whole of my duration; without any consideration of the time, whether now, or never so many myriads of ages hence.

- *Resolved*, To do whatever I think to be my duty, and most for the good and advantage of mankind in general.
- *Resolved*, To strive every week to be brought higher in religious, and to a higher exercise of grace, than I was the week before.
- *Resolved*, Never to do anything out of revenge.
- *Resolved*, To maintain the strictest temperance in eating and drinking.
- *Resolved*, To study the Scriptures so steadily, constantly, and frequently, as that I may find, and plainly perceive, myself to grow in the knowledge of the same.
- *Resolved*, Never, henceforth, till I die, to act as if I were any way my own, but entirely and altogether God's.[2]

As you can see, the resolutions in and of themselves are amazing. They were both broad and specific. They dealt with both his physical life and spiritual life. They were both personal and corporate. They covered almost every imaginable area of his life.

What is even more amazing is that he made the resolutions at all. In our day, maybe the most important lesson we learn from his resolutions comes from the simple fact that he had them, read them weekly, and spent his life trying to keep them. They speak to not only his *desire* to walk with God but his *discipline* and *determination* to walk with God. He didn't just want to walk with God, he disciplined himself to attain it (1 Tim. 4:7–10).

The men of this generation need Jonathan Edwards in countless ways, but what we need most is his resolve. We need his firm determination to walk with God and live for God. It is what made Edwards the man for his day, and it is what will make us the men for ours.

Who's the Problem?

When Elijah finally met Ahab after three long years of drought and famine, Ahab blamed Elijah. He looked at him and immediately said, "Is that you, the one ruining Israel?" (1 Kings 18:17). In Ahab's mind, Elijah was the problem. After all, he was the one who said it would not rain.

But Elijah knew better. He knew that the drought was the judgment of God on Ahab for his rebellion. Ahab had "abandoned the LORD's commands and followed the Baals" (v. 18).

Ahab and Elijah disagreed about almost everything, including whose fault the drought was. But they did agree on one thing: Israel had a problem. The nation was in trouble. The people were suffering. Something needed to change. But they did not agree on the reason for the problem—or even the problem itself.

In Ahab's mind, the primary problem was the drought. Ahab was oblivious to the fact the drought was the symptom, not the problem. The problem was rebellion, and the only solution was repentance.

Not much has changed since the days of Elijah. Almost everyone agrees there are problems. Problems in our nation, problems in the church, problems in the home. No one would argue that. The questions are: What is the problem and why does it exist?

The story of Ahab reminds us of what is always at the root of such problems: rebellious men. I understand that this can be seen as an oversimplification of very complex problems, but the truth is, the suffering of a nation, a church, and a home can almost always be traced back to unfaithful men who fail to walk in humble obedience to the Lord.

The problem in the garden was not just the deception of Eve, but the passivity of Adam. Sin entered the world because of an unfaithful man. Sin most often reigns in a home, a church, and a nation for the same reason.

In Elijah's day, as in ours, it is often those who stand for the truth who are seen as the problem. But the problem is not those who stand for the truth, but those who stand against the truth. Or worse, those who don't stand for anything. The problem is always caused by the failure of men. Not just openly rebellious men, but secretly undecided men—men with no resolve.[3]

When men, like Ahab, fail to be faithful to God and fail to stand for the things of God, everyone under their care pays the price. The lack of godliness in a man's life is never just his problem. It affects everyone around him. This is why to see any change, the change must begin with men. To turn the tide in any nation, church, or home, there must be among God's men a firm determination to walk with God and live for God. Not just desire, but resolve.

Unwavering or Wavering

After getting to the root cause of the problems in Israel, Elijah gave instructions to Ahab about what was going to happen next: "Now therefore send and gather all Israel to me at Mount Carmel, and the 450 prophets of Baal and the 400 prophets of Asherah, who eat at Jezebel's table" (v. 19 ESV).

It was about time for the showdown on Mount Carmel. One of the greatest moments in all of the Old Testament. The moment in which the gods of Baal would go against the Lord to see which one is truly God. (More about that in the next chapter.) But one of the things that makes this battle so captivating is that, before the battle began, Elijah wanted to make sure all of Israel was watching. He told Ahab to call for all the people of Israel to gather with the 850 false prophets at Mount Carmel.

The stage was set. It was almost time. Everyone was there. But first, Elijah had a word for the crowd: "Then Elijah approached all the people and said, 'How long will you waver between two opinions? If the LORD is God, follow him. But if Baal, follow him.' But the people didn't answer him a word" (v. 21).

The word *waver* is a colorful one. It refers to someone unstable—mentally, physically, spiritually, or convictionally unstable. It is someone who bounces around between two different opinions. But it's a word used in a variety of ways.

It is used in Exodus 12 to talk about the angel of the Lord "passing over" the doors that have blood on them. In other words, the angel did not remain over the door but kept moving.

The word is used in 2 Samuel 4:4 to refer to Saul's grandson who was dropped as a child and was crippled as a result. His legs did not work properly. When he walked, he was not steady, he limped back and forth. Just like the spiritual condition of Israel. This is why many translations use the word *limping* in 1 Kings 18:21.

It is also used later in 1 Kings 18:26 when the prophets of Baal were leaping around the altar trying to invoke their god to respond. It gives us a little insight into what their dancing looked like. Probably like most of ours—hard to tell if you're dancing or your legs don't work properly.

The word can be translated as *hesitate*, *falter*, *hobble*, or even *teeter*. The vision of teetering is a good one. Much like the teeter-totter on playgrounds, you go up, then down. Up, then down. Over and over again.

This word can mean a lot of things, but one thing it cannot mean is stable, secure, confident, or steady. This word would be the exact opposite of the admonition of Paul in 1 Corinthians 15:58 when he says, "Be steadfast, immovable, always excelling in the Lord's work."

It would be the opposite of Paul's frequent admonitions to "stand." We are called to stand against the spiritual forces of darkness (Eph. 6:14), "stand firm in the faith" (1 Cor. 16:13), stand firm in your freedom in Christ (Gal. 5:1), stand fast in the Lord (1 Thess. 3:8), or stand firm in one spirit with the church (Phil. 1:27).

When Elijah gathered the nation of Israel, he saw a wavering people; they were back and forth, up and down. They could not decide if they wanted to serve the Lord or Baal. What a pitiful sight.

Men are wired to hate cowardice. It goes against everything in us. Men are also wired to be disgusted by men who have no conviction, confidence, or backbone. We have no respect for those men. We don't want to be like them, and we don't like being around them. Their character is the opposite of what we think of as the character of a man. Men stand, they do not teeter.

And yet, when we look at our own spiritual lives, what do we see? Honestly. What do you see when you look at your own spiritual life? Do you see a deeply rooted man like in Psalm 1 who meditates on the Word of God, bears fruit, and prospers? Or do you look more like a man whose actual spiritual life wavers and tetters?

Do you have strong convictions about the things of the Lord? Do you have a strong desire to follow Jesus and a disciplined determination to do it? Do your commitments and calendar reflect that kind of determination?

The mission statement of our church is "Leading people to trust and follow Jesus." One of my closest pastor friends went to a new church and made their mission statement: "Leading people to *actually* trust and follow Jesus." That one word is a great addition. Many people say they trust and follow Jesus without even thinking about it. But do they *actually* trust and follow Jesus?

Are you "actually" living life with an unwavering commitment to Jesus, or are you wavering between two opinions? Can you give a strong and honest answer to this simple question, or will you, like the nation of Israel, remain silent?

Does your life *actually* look more like the resolve of Jonathan Edwards or the indecision of Israel?

More Resolve, Not More Resolutions

Many of us, rightly so, are cynical toward New Year's resolutions. I don't know of many that I have kept (or even remembered) into July. Maybe that's my lack of discipline, but I think most of you would agree that resolutions don't seem to work that well.

What we want is not more resolutions, but more resolve prompted and empowered by the Holy Spirit. We want to be men who develop a firm determination to walk with God and live for God. We are not after external change as much as internal change. We are not looking for a change in activity as much as a change in character. We don't just want to *do* better, we want to *be* better. We want a heart of resolve more than a list of resolutions. Resolutions do nothing for a man who does not have Spirit-fueled resolve.

Our Christian life begins with a decision—a decision to trust and follow Jesus. It is a decision that flows from the acknowledgment of our own sin, the brokenness of our lives, and the consequences of our sins. When we, like the prodigal son, come to our senses and realize that life outside of the Father's house is miserable, we must then decide to humble ourselves and return home.

We do this by trusting that Jesus Christ alone is the way, truth, and life (John 14:6), and the only way to be restored into right relationship with God is through Him. We must trust the work that He has already done for us in His death, burial, and resurrection, instead of trusting any works that we have done. We then call upon the name of the Lord and ask Him to save us (Rom. 10:13).

When we do this, we are declared righteous by a holy God (2 Cor. 5:21). This is called justification. It is not a process; it is a moment.

That moment of justification leads us into a life of sanctification. Sanctification is the process in which we grow to become more like Jesus. It is not a moment; it is a lifelong process. That is the process we will be in until Jesus calls us home in the moment of "glorification."

What we often fail to realize is that, although we are "saved by grace through faith" alone apart from any works that we have done (Eph. 2:8), we are sanctified by the work of the Spirit of God and our own resolve.

In 1 Timothy 4:8–10 Paul says:

> For the training of the body has limited benefit, but godliness is beneficial in every way, since it holds promise for the present life and also for the life to come. This saying is trustworthy and deserves full acceptance. For this reason we labor and strive, because we have put our hope in the living God, who is the Savior of all people, especially of those who believe.

Did you hear those words? *Labor* and *strive.* Those are the words of resolve.

Again, in Philippians 2:12–13 Paul says, "Therefore, my dear friends, just as you have always obeyed, so now, not only in my presence but even more in my absence, work out your own salvation with fear and trembling. For it is God who is working in you both to will and to work according to his good purpose." Did you hear those words? *Work out* our own salvation. That means sustained and continuous effort. Those are the words of resolve.

In Hebrews 12:14 we are told: "Pursue peace with everyone, and holiness—without it no one will see the Lord." The *pursuit* of holiness. That is resolve.

In 1 Corinthians 9:24–27 Paul paints a helpful picture of this by saying:

> Don't you know that the runners in a stadium all race, but only one receives the prize? Run in such a way to win the prize. Now everyone who competes exercises self-control in everything. They do it to receive a perishable crown, but we an imperishable crown. So I do not run like one who runs aimlessly or box like one beating the air. Instead, I discipline my body and bring it under strict control, so that after preaching to others, I myself will not be disqualified.

Did you hear it again? *Run, compete, self-control, discipline, strict control.* Those are the words of resolve.

A man of God needs grace and grit.[4] We need the enabling power of God's Spirit to give us both the desire and the power to walk with Him. Then we need the passion and perseverance it takes to fulfill the longing in our hearts to be the man God has called us to be. We cannot be the man God has called us to be without both of those.

The truth is: The undisciplined man will never become God's man. Why? Because the life of the godly is a matter of the patient acquisition of virtue.[5] You do not become the man for the day by one decision you make, but by a lifetime of decisions you make—decisions that will flow out of a heart that is resolved to be the man God has called you to be.

Look at the Broken Fence

When it comes to anxiety, Jesus instructs us to stop and look at the birds (Matt. 6:26–27). Actually. Stop, be still, and look at the birds. It's not a metaphor. It's a command. Part of the genius of this command is not only that we can learn a lesson from the birds, but the very process of stopping and looking at the birds slows us down and calms our hearts.

If stopping and looking at the birds is a command for the anxious, stopping and looking at a broken fence is the command for those who lack resolve. Proverbs 24:30–34 says:

> I went by the field of a slacker
> and by the vineyard of one lacking sense.

Thistles had come up everywhere,
weeds covered the ground,
and the stone wall was ruined.
I saw, and took it to heart;
I looked, and received instruction:
a little sleep, a little slumber,
a little folding of the arms to rest,
and your poverty will come like a robber,
and your need, like a bandit.

Charles Spurgeon has a wonderful sermon on this in which he describes the reason we must stop and look at the broken fence. He says:

> This picture of the slothful man and his garden and field overgrown with nettles and weeds represents many a man who has professed to be a Christian, but who has become slothful in the things of God. Spiritual life has withered in him. He has backslidden; he has come down from the condition of healthy spiritual energy into one of listlessness and indifference to the things of God; and while things have gone wrong within his heart and all sorts of mischiefs have come into him and grown up and seeded themselves in him, mischief is also taking place externally in his daily conduct.

> The stone wall which guarded his character is broken down, and he lies open to all evil.[6]

The broken down fence is the picture of a man who does not care for his spiritual life. A man with no resolve.

Spurgeon goes on to say:

> Our holy faith teaches a man to be decided in the cause of Christ, and to be resolute in getting rid of evil habits. "If thine eye offend thee"—wear a shade? No; "pluck it out." "If thine arm offend thee"—hang it in a sling? No; "cut it off and cast it from thee." True religion is very thorough in what it recommends. It says to us, "touch not the unclean thing." But many persons are so idle in the ways of God that they have no mind of their own: evil companions tempt them and they cannot say "*No.*" They need a stone wall made up of noes. Here are the stones, "no, no, no." Dare to be singular. Resolve to keep close to Christ. Make a stern determination to permit nothing in your life, however gainful or pleasurable, if it would dishonor the name of Jesus. Be dogmatically true, obstinately holy, immovably honest, desperately kind, fixedly upright.[7]

Without the firm determination to follow Jesus, all of our lives will be like the broken fence.

Live Today Like the Man You Want to Be Tomorrow

When I read carefully through the resolutions of Jonathan Edwards, two things stand out to me. First, his desire to make the most of every moment; the resolve to make the most of his time and take every moment seriously. Second, living in light of eternity.

- *Resolved*, To live with all my might, while I do live.
- *Resolved*, Never to lose a moment of time, but to improve it in the most profitable way I possibly can.
- *Resolved*, That I will live so, as I shall wish I had done when I come to die.
- *Resolved,* To think much, on all occasions, of my dying.[8]

Why all the emphasis on this very moment and on the very last moment? Because all of our current moments determine the man we will be in our very last moments. This is why resolve matters so much.

I would imagine that you picked up this book because, to some degree, you long to be the man for the day. You want to be ready and willing to be the person God has called you to be. You want your life to matter. You want to make an impact. You want to be an agent of change in whatever ways God has for you.

That desire is good. It's godly. If you have any hunger and thirst for righteousness, it's because God put it there. But that desire must be accompanied by discipline. Most men fail to be the men God has called them to be, not because they lack desire, but because they lack discipline.

Like Edwards, we must look at the person we want to be when we die and be resolved to do what it takes to become that person today.

If we look at any man from history who was the man for the day—a man used of God in his generation—he will be a man who at some point resolved to take seriously what matters most: his walk with Jesus Christ. Be resolved to walk with Him today.

The Man for the Day

The man for the day knows that no one accidentally becomes a man useful to God. He knows that becoming a man of God demands discipline and determination.

The man for the day has a vision of the kind of man he wants to be and then disciplines himself for that purpose. He removes things that hinder the fulfillment of that vision and adds things that help the fulfillment of it.

The man for the day knows that the areas of most importance demand the most discipline. He disciplines himself for godliness, knowing that everything else in life flows out of what is going on in his spiritual life.

Be the man for the day.

Chapter 6

Fire

Fire: Being consumed with the passionate pursuit of God's manifest presence.

WHEN ABRAHAM RECEIVED the promise of God to make him into a great nation, he gathered his family, left his home, and began walking with no idea where he was going (Gen. 12; Heb. 11:8). It was on that journey, when the Lord came to him in a vision and renewed the covenant He had made with him, that Abraham met God in the fire (Gen. 15:17).

Before Moses was called to lead the people of God out of Egypt, he was shepherding his father-in-law's sheep. It was there, on Mount Horeb in the land of Midian, that Moses met God in the fire. Moses heard the voice of God and experienced the presence of God as he removed his sandals at the burning bush (Exod. 3:2–5).

When the people of Israel were miraculously delivered from Egypt and crossed the Red Sea on dry ground, they started their journey toward the promised land. It was there, on the other side of the Red Sea, that Israel met God in the fire. The Lord led them with a pillar of fire (13:21–22) and they saw the fire on Mount Sinai (19:18).

After David sinned against the Lord by taking a census of Israel, and the Lord punished the nation by sending a plague, David built an altar to the Lord so the plague would be stopped. It was there David met the Lord in the fire that fell from heaven on the altar (1 Chron. 21:26).

When King Solomon had finished building the temple, he blessed all of Israel, prayed with his hands spread toward heaven, and prepared an offering to the Lord. It was there that Solomon met the Lord in the fire as the glory of the Lord filled the temple and fire came from heaven and consumed the sacrifice (2 Chron. 6–7).

When the Lord called Isaiah, He gave him a glorious vision of Himself, high and exalted, seated on a throne, and surrounded by the angels crying, "Holy, holy, holy is the Lord Almighty." It was there, when the Lord commissioned Isaiah, that he met God in the fire, as the seraphim touched his mouth with the burning coals from the altar (Isa. 6:1–8 TLB).

After the ascension of Jesus, 120 men and women gathered in an upper room, praying and waiting on the promise of the Holy Spirit. It was there, in that room, that they met the Lord in the fire as the Spirit came upon them and filled them (Acts 2:1–4).

When the apostle John was forced into exile on the island of Patmos, the Lord gave him a revelation of the exalted Christ. It was there, seeing Jesus with his eyes blazing, his feet glowing, and his face shining, that John met God in the fire (Rev. 1:9–20).

And it was in that same vision that John saw seven golden lampstands surrounding Jesus, which represented the church for which Jesus died (vv. 12, 20). It is there when it becomes clear, God's desire is for His people not only to meet Him in the fire but be consumed by the fire.[1]

When the Fire Fell

Imagine the scene: The 450 prophets of Baal and the 400 prophets of Asherah, brought to the nation of Israel by Jezebel, gathered on Mount Carmel ready to do battle. Hundreds of thousands of people began to appear, surrounding the mountain, anxious to know why they had been commanded to come. And there, all alone, stood one man—Elijah, the man for the day.

As the nation of Israel gathered in the presence of 850 false prophets who despised the name of the Lord, Elijah stood in front of God's people and asked them a simple question:

"How long will you waver between two opinions? If the LORD is God, follow him. But if Baal, follow him" (1 Kings 18:21a).

Their response? "But the people didn't answer him a word" (v. 21b). Maybe they remained silent because they had heard the stories of how Jezebel was systematically killing the prophets of the Lord. Maybe it was out of fear of what standing for the Lord might cost them. Maybe. But probably not.

Most likely, the people did not answer because they really could not decide who they wanted to follow. They wanted it both ways.

They wanted a little of the Lord and a little of Baal and Asherah. They had no intention of rejecting the Lord completely, but also no intention of worshiping the Lord only. They were addicted to idolatry and passivity.

Elijah knew that this lack of decision was not an option. He knew the people needed to see, in the most obvious way possible, there was only one God who must be worshiped and followed wholly, or not at all. Elijah also knew the people needed to see the absolute impotence of these false gods of Jezebel and the absolute insanity of following them.

So it was there that Elijah declared war on the lukewarm hearts of God's people and the prophets who led them astray. He was going to let the Lord preach His own sermon. A sermon they would never forget. A sermon not with words, but with fire.

Here was Elijah's proposal: Both parties get a bull. Both parties build an altar. Both parties put wood on it. Neither party puts fire on the altar. The prophets call upon the name of their god, Elijah calls upon the name of the Lord, and the "God who answers with fire, he is God" (vv. 23–24a).

Here is the genius of this proposal. Those who followed Baal believed he had control over the element of fire. Elijah was giving all the advantage to his opponents. And the people knew it.[2] The people and the prophets heard the proposal and agreed to it (v. 24b).

The prophets began to pray to Baal from morning until noon, begging him to answer. They danced around the altar while Elijah stood by and mocked them. He suggested that maybe their god could not answer because he had gone to sleep, was on a journey, or maybe he had just gone to the bathroom (v. 27).

The prophets cried louder. They cut themselves with swords and knives until blood gushed from their bodies. They raved until the sun went down, doing anything they could to get the attention of their god. Exhausted, hurt, and humiliated, they finally stopped because "no one answered, no one paid attention" (v. 29).

Now it was Elijah's turn. He gathered twelve stones, built his altar, cut up his bull, and laid wood on it. But just to make it interesting, and to further humiliate his opponents and exalt the Lord, he dug a trench around his altar and poured twelve buckets of water on it. The water filled every part of his altar. And as you know, wet wood does not burn.

Elijah came near the people and prayed:

> "Lord, the God of Abraham, Isaac, and Israel, today let it be known that you are God in Israel and I am your servant, and that at your word I have done all these things. Answer me, Lord! Answer me so that this people will know that you, the Lord, are God and that you have turned their hearts back." (vv. 36–37)

The Lord did answer: "Then the fire of the Lord fell and consumed the burnt offering and the wood and the stones and the dust, and licked up the water that was in the trench" (v. 38 ESV). It was there, with all of Israel watching, surrounded by 850 false prophets, where the people of Israel met God in the fire.

The Fire of Manifest Presence

We should not be surprised that the people met God in the fire that day. From Genesis to Revelation, God made himself known through fire. But what is the fire and what does it represent?

The simple answer is: The fire represents the manifest presence of God.

When we think about the presence of God, we tend to think only about his omnipresence. When we talk about God's omnipresence, we mean that God is in all places at all times. But that is not what the fire represents. We are not talking about his omnipresence, but his manifest presence. Not just that God is in all places at all times, but that God makes Himself known in special ways and certain times. That God will make himself known in personal, relational, and felt ways.

We believe that God is omnipresent. God is everywhere all the time and at the same time. As Psalm 139:7 says, "Where can I go to escape your Spirit? Where can I flee from your presence?"

Jeremiah declares that a man cannot hide himself in a secret place so God does not see him, for God fills the heavens and the earth (Jer. 23:24). There is no place you can go where God is not already there. God is omnipresent. What a comforting reality!

But there has to be more to the presence of God than his omnipresence. If God's presence is only about his omnipresence, how were Adam and Eve removed from God's presence in the garden (Gen. 3:20–24)? You can't be removed from God's omnipresence.

If the omnipresence is all there is, why would there be a need for a tabernacle or a temple where God's presence would dwell (Exod. 25:8)?

If God's presence is only his omnipresence, why would David say that he seeks God's presence continually (Ps. 105:4)? Why would David seek something he knows he already had?

If there is only omnipresence, how do you explain the promise of Jesus that "where two or three are gathered together in my name, I am there among them" (Matt. 18:20)?

James 4:8a says, "Draw near to God, and he will draw near to you." The promise to draw near could not be the promise of his omnipresence. There must be more to His presence.

All of these verses, and thousands more, refer to the manifest presence of God. When we talk about the manifest presence of God, we are talking about His felt presence; His relational presence; His personal presence; His experienced, evident, and undeniable presence.[3]

The omnipresence of God is impersonal. God is omnipresent at a Buddhist temple and a Muslim mosque. His omnipresence does not change. You cannot have more or less of his omnipresence. Yet throughout the Bible people have longed for more of God's presence.

A. W. Tozer said, "The presence and the manifestation of God's presence are not the same. There can be one without the other. God is here when we are wholly unaware of it. He is manifest only when and as we are aware of His presence."[4]

When Adam and Eve were removed from the garden, they lost something real. Something personal. Something intimate. Something felt. They lost the manifest presence of God. And it is that which our hearts have longed for ever since. We long for God to be real, personal, known, and experienced.

When David says that his soul pants for God like a deer pants for water, or that his soul thirsts for God like in a dry and weary land where there is no water, he is longing for the manifest presence of God (Pss. 42; 64). He wants God to be real and known and intimate.

If we are content only to know God's omnipresence and fail to seek His manifest presence, we miss what God has created us for: intimacy with Him. God created us for His manifest presence. For relational intimacy. For closeness. For oneness.

The reason God so often meets men in the fire is because God is communicating what we seem to miss: God will never use a man until he meets God in the fire. If a man does not know the manifest presence of God, he cannot be a man used of God.

Men on Fire

Of all the seven churches who received a word from God in Revelation 2–3, God was most disgusted with the church of Laodicea (Rev. 3:14–22). That church made God nauseated to the point of throwing up. But why?

The answer is found back in Revelation 1. Revelation 1 could be titled "Man on Fire." John received a vision of Jesus, from head to toe as a man on fire. And He was surrounded by seven lampstands, which are bowls of fire. These lampstands represent the church (v. 20). This means that God designed the church to be ablaze with the glory of Jesus Christ. Or to say it another way, to be ablaze with the fire of His manifest presence.

The church was created to be the visible presence of Jesus on earth. And how can the church be the visible presence of Jesus on earth unless it is full of the fire of God's manifest presence? If Jesus is on fire, His church must be on fire.

The reason the lukewarm church makes God sick is because the church was designed to be ablaze! It was created to be ablaze with the fire of God's manifest presence. The church was to be so filled with the Spirit of God that it manifested the fire of Jesus Himself in Revelation 1.

But the church in Laodicea was lukewarm. It was not cold. It was not hot. That church was just like the people of Israel who stood before Elijah and could not decide if they wanted to follow the Lord or Baal.

When speaking about the church of Laodicea, John Stott says, "Perhaps none of the seven letters is more appropriate to the church at the beginning of the twenty-first century than this. It describes vividly the respectable nominal rather sentimental skin-deep religiosity which is so widespread among us today. Our Christianity is flabby and anemic. We appear to have taken a lukewarm bath of religion."[5] What a true and sad indictment on the modern church.

When I was growing up, it seemed like every pastor and student pastor used to talk about being "on fire for God." I don't hear that much anymore. It's probably because the phrase became overused and lost its effectiveness. But understood in the context of Revelation 1–3, there may be no better phrase we could use to call out the men of this generation.

To be on fire for God means to know, experience, and be filled with God's presence. It means to have daily encounters with the living God that are so intimate that the fire of His presence rubs off on you and is felt by all those who are around you.

In the same way that Moses's face glowed when he came off the mountain after meeting with God (Exod. 34:29–35), every man of God must glow with the fire that only comes from being in His presence.

The world does not need more lukewarm men who nauseate God. We don't need lukewarm church members or lukewarm fathers or lukewarm husbands. We don't need a Christianity that is flabby and anemic. We need men who will not be satisfied until they are ablaze with God's presence. We need men who understand God's manifest presence and seek it continually. We need men on fire.

Meeting God in the Fire

When you look back at all the men who met God in the fire, they all had one thing in common: They knew they had met with God. None of them wondered if it was God. They might have been in awe of what happened, but they were not confused as to Whom they had met. When they met God in the fire, God was real to them.

This seems to be the problem with so many men today. God is not real to them. They can play the game. They can speak the language. But they cannot speak personally of what it means to meet with God. The reason there are so few men on fire is because they don't personally know what it means to meet with God.

At the most basic level, meeting God in the fire means spending time in His presence. The glow on Moses's face was the glow that could only have come from meeting God in the fire. God is calling you to the same place he called Moses. He is calling you into His presence. He is calling you into intimacy. He is calling you into closeness. He wants to make Himself real to you. He wants to speak to you. He wants you to be able to speak with personal experience about what it means to know Him.

God is calling you to give Him the time and space that is needed to find out, once and for all, that God is not distant, but real. He is not cold; He is on fire. He is not emotionally numb; He is passionately in love with you. But you will not know any of that until you sit alone, Bible in hand, ready to hear and receive from God.

One of the greatest calls to meet with God is from the heart of David in Psalm 24:

> Who may ascend the mountain of the LORD?
> Who may stand in his holy place?
> The one who has clean hands and a pure heart,
> who has not appealed to what is false,
> and who has not sworn deceitfully.

> He will receive blessing from the LORD,
> and righteousness from the God of his salvation.
> Such is the generation of those who inquire of
> him,
> who seek the face of the God of Jacob. *Selah*
> (vv. 3–6)

Meeting God in the fire always starts with desire. It starts when we feel as nauseated about our lukewarm hearts as God does. It starts with a hunger and thirst for righteousness that God has put in our hearts and longs to satisfy (Matt. 5:6).

It moves from desire to purity. It means confessing any known sin, turning from that sin, and receiving the forgiveness of the Lord. When John says, "If we confess our sins, he is faithful and righteous to forgive us our sins and to cleanse us from all unrighteousness" (1 John 1:9), he is talking to believers.

Meeting God in the fire moves from desire to purity to pursuit. As Psalm 24 says, such is the generation of those who seek Him. We make Jesus a priority. We discipline ourselves for godliness. We actually seek God. We seek His presence. We don't want to know about Him, we want to know Him.

The goal of spending time in His presence is not checking off a few boxes on your daily Bible reading plan. The goal is that God would no longer feel distant, but close. That God would feel real, personal, intimate, and known. In other words, meeting God in the fire is to experience the manifest presence of God. That is what you were created for. You were created to be ablaze with the presence of God. You cannot settle for less.

A Passion for Presence

The vision statement of our church states: "Our Vision is to be the visible presence of Jesus in our community, a healthy and growing family of faith that is passionate about experiencing, enjoying, and expanding God's presence to every neighbor and every nation."

The vision of our church is to raise up a generation of passionate people. This matters as deeply to me as anything else in my life. More specifically, I want to raise up a generation that is passionate for the presence of God.

And the way you create a passionate people is not primarily through passionate songs and passionate sermons, but through leading people into the presence of God. When people get passionate about experiencing and enjoying God's presence, the red-hot passion of God will fill them and overflow from them.

We have defined *Fire* in this chapter as: "being consumed with the passionate pursuit of God's manifest presence." Passionate pursuit.

In the simplest terms, I am writing this book to "fire men up!" To put inside of their hearts a burning passion for God. A passion to be used by God. A passion to be the men God has called them to be. To call men to settle for nothing less than being the man for the day.

A man cannot be on fire unless he meets God in the fire. And you cannot manufacture this. You might fool some people, but you will not fool God. And honestly, you aren't really fooling as many people as you think you are. If you have not met God in the fire, people can tell.

But once you meet God in the fire, you will never be the same. This is true of every man whom we listed. They were never the same after their encounter with God. They had gotten a taste of His voice. They had gotten a taste of His presence. And after that, nothing else would satisfy them but God. They had gotten a taste of the real God.

This is an important distinction. We are not looking for a dramatic moment, but a daily pursuit. God most often transforms our lives not from a dramatic moment when fire falls, but from daily moments in which the fire falls. The pursuit of fire is the pursuit of God.

Remember This

As you begin to seek the manifest presence of God, there are a few things you must remember. First, the greatest need of your life is the manifest presence of God. Everything flows from His presence.[6] You will always be lukewarm, at best, without His presence. There is nothing that matters more than His presence. Once you taste it, there is nothing you will want more. Nothing else will satisfy you. It is the greatest need of your life and will become the greatest joy of your life.

Second, God wants to make Himself known to you. What continues to bring me back to this pursuit over and over again is the simple promise of James 4:8a: "Draw near to God, and he will draw near to you." God wants to come near. God longs for nothing more than to bring us back into the place He created us to be—the place of His manifest presence. He makes Himself known to those who want to know Him.

Third, when God gives you a desire for Him, it is always an invitation to the fire. Maybe God is igniting a desire in your heart right now to know Him more deeply and intimately. If He is, pursue it! Go after it! That desire is God summoning you to Himself. He has something He wants to say to you. He has something He wants to do in you. Draw near to Him. Again, A. W. Tozer said:

> The Presence and the manifestation of the Presence are not the same. There can be the one without the other. God is here when we are wholly unaware of it. He is *manifest* only when and as we are aware of His Presence. On our part there must be surrender to the Spirit of God, for His work it is to show us the Father and the Son. If we co-operate with Him in loving obedience God will manifest Himself to us, and that manifestation will be the difference between a nominal Christian life and a life radiant with the light of His face.[7]

Don't settle for anything less than a life that radiates with the glow that can only come from His presence. That's the only kind of men we need and the only kind who will be the man for the day.

The Man for the Day

The man for the day knows the difference between the omnipresence and the manifest presence of God. He is not satisfied with anything less than experiencing God's manifest presence.

The man for the day seeks God's presence continually. He longs to meet with God. He loves God's presence. He knows that everything good in his life flows from time in God's presence.

The man for the day is not satisfied with a lukewarm heart. He knows that he was created to be ablaze with the fire of God's manifest presence. And he knows that the fire is only kindled in intimacy with God.

Be the man for the day!

Chapter 7

Repentance

Repentance: Waging war on the sin that is waging war against you.

MY WIFE AND I just celebrated twenty years of marriage. As I look back on those twenty years, I can't help but to think about one of the defining moments of our marriage that happened around year nine. Andrea said she needed to talk to me, so we sat on the side of the bed to talk. Everything seemed to be going well, so the "we need to talk" comment didn't have me worried.

Andrea began to share, with tears flowing down her facc, how deeply I had hurt her over the years by my harsh words and tone, and how I continued to do so. I can honestly say, I was shocked. I had never struggled with outbursts of anger, name-calling, or harsh words. I tend to boil internally, not externally. I had no idea what she was talking about.

She began to gently and lovingly show me something about myself I had never seen before. She pointed out that almost every evening when I came home from work, I came home grumpy, irritable, and critical. I have a firm belief that the temperature of a man's heart determines the temperature of a man's home. The temperature of my heart when I came home was affecting everyone. But I didn't realize it.

But it was more than that. She told me how often I would come home and make critical comments about the house, the kids, or our finances. I would talk like nothing was going well and most of our life felt like a mess. I would talk that way because that's how I felt most of the time.

What I didn't realize is that everything I was saying was in some way directed toward her. My words that were coming out of my own sense of failure made her feel like a failure. Every day when I came home from work I would act and speak in such a way that I was crushing my wife's soul.

A few years ago, I shared this story at a men's event and immediately after the event a man came directly to me and said that I had perfectly described the way he came home at night and the way his wife felt. From that moment on, I have noticed more and more men struggling with this attitude. I don't think I'm alone in this. I don't think Andrea is alone in this either. I wonder how many wives are being crushed by it?

I spent a long time thinking through why I acted this way, not only to help myself, but to help other men. I do believe that some of it has to do with pressure and stress at work, the feeling of inadequacy at home, and the sense that no matter how much we do, it's never enough. Those things are real, but they are symptoms of the problem, not the problem.

For me, the root problem was my own sense of internal defeat. I was grumpy, irritable, critical, and unkind because I was carrying a deep sense of guilt, condemnation, and defeat in my own heart due to unconfessed and hidden sin. I don't think I'm alone in this, either.

If a kid is constantly bullied and told he's no good, at some point he will start to believe it. He will walk around with his head down, just hoping no one sees or notices him. He will remain quiet, stay to himself, and lose all sense of who he really is, or he will bully others and bring others down with him. As the old saying goes, "Hurt people hurt people."

If a Christian man is walking around with unconfessed sin, it will eat him alive. It will destroy him from the inside out. It will not only kill his soul, but those souls of everyone around him. It's a story I've heard and seen played out repeatedly. It's the one that was playing out in my home.

In order for men to learn to be the men God has called them to be, they must learn how to turn from sin. They must learn to repent, and repent often.

Repent!

The word *repent* is often said to be the first word of the gospel. According to Matthew 4:17, the first words of Jesus's public ministry were: "Repent, because the kingdom of heaven has come near." This was the first command of His ministry. And it is a command.

Jesus demanded James and John leave their father and their fishing nets (v. 21). The woman at the well was called to leave her immoral lifestyle (John 4). He demanded Zacchaeus leave his life of crime (Luke 19:1–10). He demanded the rich young ruler leave his wealth (Mark 10:17–22). Jesus has always demanded repentance as the means by which we begin our journey with Him.[1]

When declaring the gospel to the philosophers in Athens, Paul said, "Therefore, having overlooked the times of ignorance, God now commands all people everywhere to repent, because he has set a day when he is going to judge the world in righteousness by the man he has appointed. He has provided proof of this to everyone by raising him from the dead" (Acts 17:30–31).

There is no salvation without repentance. Jesus said, "Unless you repent, you will all perish as well" (Luke 13:5). The judgment of God and full outpouring of His wrath await all those who do not repent. This is why the calling to repentance was the purpose for which Christ came. He said, "I have not come to call the righteous, but sinners to repentance" (5:32). And this is why the commission for every believer until He returns is to ensure that "repentance for forgiveness of sins will be proclaimed in his name to all the nations, beginning at Jerusalem" (24:47).

No one can be saved without repentance. Jesus demands it and the gospel requires it. But what role does repentance play after salvation?

Let's go back to the church at Laodicea in Revelation 3. Jesus intended for the church to be the place in which the fire of His presence was both experienced and expanded, yet the church in Laodicea was lukewarm. They had lost the fire of God's manifest presence. And their lack of fire made Jesus want to vomit. So, what should they do? How could they become a people filled with the fire of God's presence once again?

Jesus gives the answer as clearly as possible. He says, "As many as I love, I rebuke and discipline. So be zealous and repent" (Rev. 3:19). Being lukewarm is a sin. It always has been. And the response to sin is always the same: repentance. As long as we struggle with sin, we will need to repent.

Writing to believers, the apostle John says, "If we say, 'We have no sin,' we are deceiving ourselves, and the truth is not in us. If we confess our sins, he is faithful and righteous to forgive us our sins and to cleanse us from all unrighteousness" (1 John 1:8–9). The ongoing reality of sin makes turning from sin an ongoing necessity.

James, the brother of Jesus, also writing to believers, says, "Draw near to God, and he will draw near to you. Cleanse your hands, sinners, and purify your hearts, you double-minded" (James 4:8). In order for us to experience and enjoy the fullness of God's presence, we must continually cleanse our hands and hearts through repentance.

I love the way Richard Owen Roberts describes this. He said:

> Repentance makes the path straight between the Lord and the repenting person. Repentance is like clearing a highway of holiness to and from God. . . . Apart from repentance, the Lord will

> not make His way to us. Making straight the way of the Lord is always a prelude to His coming. In repentance we clear our path to God; in granting us this repentance, God clears His path to us.[2]

If we want to ascend the hill of the Lord, experience His presence, know Him, enjoy Him, and be used by Him, we must come to Him with clean hands and a pure heart (Ps. 24:4). The only way to do that is through repentance. This is why repentance is essential to the life of any man who wants to know and be used by God. Without repentance, a man will never experience the fullness of life God has for him and will never become the man for the day. Instead, his life will manifest the brokenness that comes from unconfessed sin.

Falling on Your Face

When Elijah stood before the people and asked them to choose who they would worship, they said nothing (1 Kings 18:21). They didn't hate the Lord; they just didn't love Him exclusively. Yet they knew the Lord demanded exclusive love (Deut. 6:5). But they, much like the church at Laodicea, wanted a little of the Lord and a little of the world. They wanted to worship the Lord and the other gods brought in by Jezebel. This is why they stood there undecided.

They knew that they were a people called to worship the Lord. In their minds, Baal and Asherah offered things the Lord didn't. They thought they needed Baal and Asherah for issues of weather and fertility. Among other things, the worship of Baal and Asherah involved something they wanted but the Lord did not permit: ritual prostitution.

But when Elijah challenged these false prophets to a public duel, their gods were publicly humiliated and revealed for what they really were—impotent and imaginary.

When the people saw the Lord respond by sending fire from heaven, the people responded in the only way appropriate: "When all the people saw it, they fell facedown and said, 'The Lord, he is God! The Lord, he is God!'" (1 Kings 18:39).

There are many examples of people falling on their faces before God, especially when specific people or an entire nation encountered God's presence (Gen. 17:1–3; Num. 14:5; Josh. 5:14; 1 Chron. 21:16).

When Solomon dedicated the temple, the fire of the Lord fell, the people met God, and they immediately bowed down.

> When Solomon finished praying, fire descended from heaven and consumed the burnt offering and the sacrifices, and the glory of the Lord filled the temple. The priests were not able to enter the Lord's temple because the glory of the Lord filled the temple of the Lord. All the Israelites were watching when the fire descended and the glory of the Lord came on the temple. They bowed down on the pavement with their faces to the ground. They worshiped and praised the Lord: For he is good, for his faithful love endures forever. (2 Chron. 7:1–3)

The same thing happened when the fire of God fell in 1 Kings 18. When God manifested His presence, the people became aware of His holiness and the depth of their sin. They knew that He was God and they knew He must be worshiped. And their immediate response to those realities was to fall with their faces to the ground (v. 39).

In that moment, the people changed their actions and turned from idols to the living God. They turned from half-hearted affection to whole-hearted devotion, falling to the ground and declaring the supremacy of the Lord was an act of humility. It was an act of sorrow. It was an act of worship. It was an act of awe. It was an act the Bible calls repentance.[3]

When you find yourself in God's presence, coming face-to-face with the reality of your sin and His holiness, falling on your face in worship and repentance is the only appropriate response.

As much as we think about the foolishness of following gods like Baal and Asherah, the reality is, we all turn to idols. We just call them by different names. It could be family, work, sports, sex, lust, ambition, hobbies, the approval of others, or money. Anything that has our full attention and affection is what we worship. And anytime we find our hearts drawn away from God by lesser things, we must respond with genuine repentance.

But what does that look like practically? What does it mean to repent?

What Is Repentance?

At a student camp I once heard someone give a passionate testimony about how they met the Lord and did a complete 360. I appreciate the sincere passion, but I'm pretty sure they meant a 180. When we think about repentance, this is what we tend to think about: turning away from sin and turning toward Christ. But there is more to it than that. It might help to think of repentance with four words: *conviction*, *contrition*, *confession*, and *change*.

Repentance begins with conviction. Conviction is a supernatural work of the Holy Spirit by which we realize what we have done is wrong. Conviction is the knowledge that we are moving in the wrong direction and need to turn back. It is not just the fear of being caught, it is the awareness that our actions broke the law—and the heart—of God. When the Spirit convicts us of sin, we see our actions for what they really are: a sin against a holy God (Ps. 51:4; John 16:8).

Second, repentance includes contrition. If conviction is our awareness of sin, contrition is our grief over sin. When we feel contrition, we not only know that our sin has grieved God's Spirit, but that it grieves ours. Contrition is hatred for sin. Contrition is a mixture of sorrow and disgust.

It is seen in the declaration by the prophet Joel when he said, "Even now—this is the Lord's declaration—turn to me with all your heart, with fasting, weeping, and mourning. Tear your hearts, not just your clothes, and return to the Lord your God. For he is gracious and compassionate, slow to anger, abounding in faithful love, and he relents from sending disaster" (Joel 2:12–13).

James is calling for contrition when he says, "Draw near to God, and he will draw near to you. Cleanse your hands, sinners, and purify your hearts, you double-minded. Be miserable and mourn and weep. Let your laughter be turned to mourning and your joy to gloom" (James 4:8–9). In other words, stop taking your sin lightly. Let it break your heart.

We feel contrition when we feel deep hatred for sin and a longing to be rid of it. But repentance is more than just emotion. Repentance is action. Those actions are the next two words.

Third, true repentance leads to confession. If we are truly sorry for our sin and truly long to be rid of our sin, we must confess our sin. Confession is when we are honest with God and others about the sins we have committed. Confession not only acknowledges that what we have done is wrong, but that we need help we don't have.

If you are wondering if confession is really necessary, here is what David said about his sin with Bathsheba in Psalm 32:

> When I kept silent, my bones became brittle
> from my groaning all day long.
> For day and night your hand was heavy on me;
> my strength was drained
> as in the summer's heat. *Selah*
> Then I acknowledged my sin to you
> and did not conceal my iniquity.
> I said, "I will confess my transgressions to the
> LORD,"
> and you forgave the guilt of my sin. *Selah*
> (vv. 3–5)

Proverbs 28:13 says, "The one who conceals his sins will not prosper, but whoever confesses and renounces them will find mercy."

Covering up your sin is the opposite of repentance. Repentance humbly confesses sin and receives the gracious help of God and others. Hiding sin is pride and makes it impossible to be delivered from sin because it brings on the opposition of God (James 4:6). When a man hides his sin, he not only harms himself and others but also removes the possibility of deliverance.

The only pathway to freedom from sin is the pathway of honesty and humility. So many men remain in sin because of the simple refusal to get honest about their sin with God *and* others. But true healing and deliverance from sin demand honest confession. Without confession, there will be no deliverance.

If you have confessed over and over to God, but have seen no change, you need to confess that sin to someone else. While repentance before God is sufficient for salvation, it is not sufficient for sanctification. John says it this way:

> This is the message we have heard from him and declare to you: God is light, and there is absolutely no darkness in him. If we say, "We have fellowship with him," and yet we walk in darkness, we are lying and are not practicing the truth. If we walk in the light as he himself is in the light, we have fellowship with one another, and the blood of Jesus his Son cleanses us from all sin. If we say, "We have no sin," we are deceiving ourselves, and the truth is

> not in us. If we confess our sins, he is faithful and righteous to forgive us our sins and to cleanse us from all unrighteousness. (1 John 1:5–9)

Confession to others is what will ultimately bring change. It is in that honesty and humility that the grace of God and the help of others work together to deliver you from that besetting sin. Walking in the light means walking in honesty before God and others.

On a practical note, if a man refuses to be honest and humble about his sin with others, he will be much more likely to continue to struggle with no real deliverance. However, if a man has no secrets and learns to confess regularly, he is far less likely to have a major moral failure.

Finally, repentance demands change. By the power of the Holy Spirit within us, we make every possible effort to fight and flee from sin. We take real, practical, often dramatic steps away from sin and toward holiness. In the same way that Joseph ran from Potiphar's wife, we run with all our might away from sin (Gen. 39).

When Jesus says, "If your right eye causes you to sin, gouge it out and throw it away" (Matt. 5:29) and "If your right hand causes you to sin, cut if off and throw it away" (v. 30), He is showing both the seriousness of sin and the dramatic steps we must take to rid ourselves of sin. Although we do not literally gouge out an eye or cut off a hand, we might get rid of our cell phones, get off social media, take a break from the television, or any other action that might keep us from sin. True repentance takes the hatred for sin and turns it into specific action against sin.

Most men fail to be delivered from besetting sin for lack of confession and lack of change. They may feel conviction and even contrition, but they fail to repent fully by failing to do the hard work of confession and change. Which means, although they don't want to sin, they don't really want to be rid of sin either.

If you confess without specific and practical steps of change, you will not be free from sin. And if you take specific and practical steps to change without confession, you will not be free from sin. True repentance starts with God's Spirit making us aware that we have sinned and is completed when we take the radical actions to get rid of that sin by the power of the same Spirit.

Worked In and Worked Out

Every step of repentance is initiated and empowered by the Holy Spirit of God. Without the Holy Spirit we will never experience true conviction or contrition and will never move toward confession and change. The Holy Spirit is the source of all this. But that does not absolve us from any responsibility. Repentance demands the supernatural work of the Holy Spirit and the hard work of your Holy Spirit–infused will.

Paul tells the Philippians, "Therefore, my dear friends, just as you have always obeyed, so now, not only in my presence but even more in my absence, work out your own salvation with fear and trembling. For it is God who is working in you both to will and to work according to his good purpose" (Phil. 2:12–13).

When the Holy Spirit works conviction and contrition in your heart, you respond with strenuous, diligent, ongoing effort to work out what the Spirit has worked in. The Holy Spirit does not cut off our hand if it causes us to stumble, we do (Matt. 5:29–30). If we acknowledge what the Spirit has worked in—namely, conviction and contrition—but we do not respond with confession and action, we will never see any real change.

When it comes to dealing with sin, we do not "let go and let God." We don't just rest in what Jesus has done. We don't just remember the gospel. We don't just pray that the Lord will deliver us. We fight, with all of our might, as if our soul depends on it. Because it does!

You must not only hate your sin; you must hate it enough to want to get rid of it. That hatred for sin and desire to be free must drive you to take radical action if necessary.

It might be helpful to think about repentance as a weapon of war. Satan is waging a war against your soul (1 Pet. 2:11). He does not relent. He does not take a break. He will not be content until he robs you of every bit of power, joy, life, and usefulness he can. He does not play fair. He hates you and your family. He wants nothing more than to destroy all of it.

And although he cannot send the believer to hell, he can make him almost powerless and useless until he gets to heaven. That's his goal. And one of the primary ways he does this is to get us to take sin lightly. He wants us to act like life is peacetime, not wartime, and as a result, get us to stop fighting the Enemy that constantly waits to destroy us.

When we fall into sin, repentance is the way we restore our right fellowship with God and others. Repentance is saying, "I refuse to let the Enemy win. I refuse to walk in darkness. I refuse to let my friends, family, and church suffer because of my lack of honesty. I am going to wage war on sin through repentance!"

We will all lose battles. But repentance keeps us from losing the war. The men who have major moral falls don't actually have major moral falls. They just have one fall we all see after a thousand falls we didn't see. Don't take sin lightly. Wage war on it.

Fighting *for* Something

The story of Achan in Joshua 7 has always been a sobering one for me. Achan sinned, hid his sin, lied about his sin, and as a result, was killed because of his sin. But the most sobering part of his story was the effect of his sin on others. Not only were thirty-six men killed in battle because of his sin, his entire family was killed because of his sin. Never underestimate the rippling effects of your sin.

The rippling effects of sin should terrify us. That alone should motivate us to remain pure and clean before God and others. But we can't just spend our lives fighting against something. We need to fight *for* something. We don't fight sin just because we are afraid of the consequences; we fight sin because we long for the fullness of

God's blessing on our life! We are not only fighting for our life, but for our friends, our family, and our church.

Jesus came that we might have life and life abundantly (John 10:10). God's desire is that we experience the fullness of His life in us by His Spirit. He wants His life, like rivers of living water, to continually flow in us and through us, not only satisfying our souls, but giving life to others (7:37–39). This is the abundant life! God, by His Spirit, allowing us to experience the life we were created to experience, as we are filled with His Spirit. Our souls satisfied and others blessed by the life flowing from us.

Sin always hinders the life of God in you. And in order to keep the life of God flowing, those rivers of living water that flood your soul and pour out to bless others must continually keep your heart clean through repentance.

Fear the consequences of unconfessed sin. They are real. They cannot be overestimated. But more than that, fight sin and continually repent of sin because there is nothing better in all of life than the joy of intimacy with God. There is no more satisfying life than the life in which God's Spirit is flowing through us. Fight sin because you believe by faith that Jesus is always better.

Why Men Must Repent

When we walk in sin and fail to deal with that sin through repentance, we feel defeated. And that internal feeling of defeat carries over into every area of a man's life. Normally, when a man is angry with his wife and kids, it's because he's angry at himself. A man's grumpiness and resentment often flow from his own frustration with himself.

This is what the devil wants to do to the men of this generation. He wants to bully you until you believe that God can never use you. He wants you to walk around defeated, convinced that your life cannot matter. The primary way he does this is by keeping you from getting honest about your sin through repentance. He wants to fill you with fear and make you run and hide. The last thing he wants is for you to come clean.

The saddest reality of allowing your sin to defeat you is that waiting for you, at all times, is a God who is ready to clean you, change you, and fill you with the fullness of His Spirit. There is nothing this generation needs more than men who are willing to do the hard work of repentance, being right with God, full of God, and useful to God.

This book is about being a useful man. Hear this: A clean man is a useful man (2 Tim. 2:20–22). The man for the day is a man who is ready and willing to deal with his sin because he believes that God wants to use him. And God does!

The Man for the Day

The man for the day knows the devastating effects of unconfessed sin. He knows that his sin is not just his problem, but has a rippling effect on others.

The man for the day is honest about his struggles with sin. He makes repentance a regular part of his life. When he feels convicted of sin, he responds by immediately confessing that sin.

The man for the day is resolved to fight sin daily. He does not tolerate sin, but wages war on it. He hates sin and the consequences of that sin on his life and the lives of others.

The man for the day is not just fighting against sin, but for the abundant life in Jesus that comes from clean hands and a pure heart.

Be the man for the day!

Chapter 8

Anger

Anger: Being deeply bothered by what bothers God and responding in a godly way.

WHEN I WAS in elementary school, my father left the pastorate and began a ministry as a traveling evangelist. As a result, he wasn't home often, but he was sensitive to this and did all he could to make up for it. He wrote me letters, called to talk, and often took me with him. We also had a standing lunch every Saturday before he left home. Those were special moments to me. I don't have specific memories of many of those lunches, but there is one I will never forget.

At a table not far from us was a family of five. The father looked like an oil rig worker, which is possible since this happened in Oklahoma in the mid-1980s. He was big and rough, with dirty clothes, dirty hands, and a red neck. Whatever he did, he worked hard for a living.

What I remember most is the fierceness of his anger. My dad had his back turned to this man, but I was facing him. This man spoke with deep anger and hostility toward his wife and kids. He had no patience, no kindness, and no apparent love for any of them. Every word he spoke was harsh and demeaning.

It wasn't just his words. It was the fire in his eyes, the redness of his face, and the strength of his hands. I watched as he grabbed the arms of his kids and threw them around. His wife just remained silent. She was terrified of him. And so was I.

I distinctly remember being scared. I was afraid that he would turn that anger toward me if he saw me looking at him. But I couldn't help it. I had never seen anything like it before. If he was like this in public, imagine what he was like in private. I couldn't imagine living in his house, and I felt heartbroken for the small children that had to.

Directly across from me was another angry man. He wasn't angry when we walked in, but he was angry now. When I wasn't looking at the angry man across the room, I was looking back at the increasingly angry man across the table. His face was also getting red. I could see him growing more and more bothered by what he heard going on behind him. I could see him notice the fear in my eyes. And then, without any warning, he stood up, turned around, and walked directly toward the man's table.

This happened more than thirty-five years ago, and I remember every detail. My father walked to the table, stood right over this man as he was seated, and told him, in no uncertain terms, that he knew a lot of powerful people in the state and would ensure that his kids were taken away from him if he ever talked to them like that again.

To this day I can't believe a fight didn't break out. A fight that I'm fairly confident I would have watched my dad lose! I think this father was so stunned that he didn't know what to do. But for some reason, for that moment, the man's anger subsided.

This is a story of two angry men. Both of them responded to their situations with anger. But the two types of anger could not be more different.

One man's anger terrified me. One man's anger comforted me. One man's anger made me feel scared. One man's anger made me feel safe. One was disturbing, and one was comforting. One felt wrong, and one felt right.

I still remember the anger of that father, and it still grieves me. I still remember the anger of my father, and it still makes me feel loved and protected. My father's anger was good, and although I couldn't have described it at the time, I knew it was good.

Angry Men

As I recounted the story above, I was surprised by how much emotion it brought up in me. It not only stirred up love, respect, and gratitude for my dad but also stirred up the heartbreaking reality of how many families are destroyed and wives and children harmed by an angry father. I can't think of anything less manly and more cowardly than a man who hurts his family with angry words and actions.

It reminds me of the countless conversations I've had with families who live in a home with an angry man. Those situations fill me with the same anger my father felt. There are few things more destructive than an angry man. Not just the kind of anger that manifests itself in outbursts or rage, but the anger that resides deep inside many of us.

Every man struggles with anger to some degree. We all have an anger problem. Everyone experiences anger. Most people have more anger than they even realize.

Anger can manifest itself in yelling, throwing, hitting, and red-faced fits of rage. Anger can also manifest in brooding and silence. Most resentment, bitterness, bickering, defensiveness, withdrawal, irritability, avoidance, indifference, and complaining are all forms of anger. All of those are hurtful—not just to our own souls, but to everyone in their path.[1]

I have seen over the years the depth of resentment and anger that I can feel. For me, it manifests itself in ice-cold silence. And as is often said, the opposite of love is not hate, but indifference. The indifference that flows out of my anger can be the loudest silence you have ever heard.

When we hear stories of hate crimes, abuse, insurrection, street fights, carjackings, or even church conflict, most of that is an overflow of deep-seated anger that finally rose to the top. We seem to be surrounded by men who are like time bombs just waiting to blow. I am worried about this generation of angry men.

Nothing will destroy a church, a family, or a nation more than angry men. We know this. We've all seen this. And we must do something about this.

Do Not Be Angry!

We are all familiar with the admonition not to let the sun go down on your anger. But this is more than just good advice. The verses say, ". . . Don't let the sun go down on your anger, and don't give the devil an opportunity" (Eph. 4:26–27). The word *opportunity* is often translated as "foothold." Unresolved anger is like leaving an open door in which the Enemy can come in and take ground in your heart. If the Enemy is looking for a way in, anger is always an open door.

In Galatians 5, Paul contrasts the fruit of the Spirit with the works of the flesh:

> Now the works of the flesh are obvious: sexual immorality, moral impurity, promiscuity, idolatry, sorcery, hatreds, strife, jealousy, outbursts of anger, selfish ambitions, dissensions, factions, envy, drunkenness, carousing, and anything similar. I am warning you about these things—as I warned you before—that those who practice such things will not inherit the kingdom of God. (vv. 19–21)

Anger and its various manifestations, are clearly works of the flesh that are in direct opposition to the work of God.

In 1 Timothy 2, as Paul addresses the men of the church, he says, "Therefore, I want the men in every place to pray, lifting up holy hands without anger or argument" (v. 8). Isn't it interesting that the only sin Paul addresses with men is that of anger and the arguments that stem from it?

When Paul leaves Titus in Crete to fix the highly dysfunctional church there, he tells him that the first thing he must do is find godly men and put them in leadership (Titus 1:5). Paul then describes the kind of men to look for: "he must be blameless, not arrogant, not hot-tempered, not an excessive drinker, not a bully, not greedy for money, but hospitable, loving what is good, sensible, righteous, holy, self-controlled" (vv. 7–8). The man God can use is the man who can control his anger.

The reason is simple: Sinful anger never produces righteousness. "My dear brothers and sisters, understand this: Everyone should be quick to listen, slow to speak, and slow to anger, for human anger does not accomplish God's righteousness" (James 1:19–20). That's a profound verse. Sinful anger can never produce righteousness.

Think about the implications of this truth in every area of your life. If you want to be a man used of God, a man who leads and loves his family well, a man who is faithful in his church, you must deal with sinful anger. Unrighteous anger will never produce any righteousness. It will always bring harm, not good.

All of that to say: Anger is more dangerous than we can ever imagine. Even when we keep silent about it, unresolved anger is like bitterness—it will always spring up and always hurt others (Heb. 12:15). The anger in your heart is a battle you must fight and a battle you must win. That anger will hinder every good work God wants to do in your life. It must be defeated by the power of the Holy Spirit.

But that leaves us with these questions: If unrighteous anger only bears the fruit of unrighteousness, is there a righteous anger that bears the fruit of righteousness? Is there an anger that is good, right, and holy? Is there an anger, like the anger of my father that day, that should be present? And if so, what is it?

Anger, Famines, and Slaughtered Prophets

Before Elijah comes on the scene, we are introduced to King Ahab. His father was evil. His grandfather was evil. His great-grandfather was evil. Every king before him was evil. So evil, that by the time you get to Ahab you just assume it couldn't get any worse. Unfortunately, that wasn't the case.

We are first introduced to Ahab with these words: "But Ahab son of Omri did what was evil in the LORD's sight more than all who were before him. . . . Ahab did more to anger the LORD God of Israel than all the kings of Israel who were before him" (1 Kings 16:30, 33b). Ahab was evil, and his evil angered the Lord. The Lord's anger was manifested in His righteous judgment on Ahab and the people of Israel. If anger does not produce righteousness, how do we explain an angry God? A phrase from the book of Exodus helps answer that question.

In Exodus 32, while Moses was on Mount Sinai receiving the law of God, the people made a golden calf and worshiped it. The Lord was angry. He was not frustrated or irritated. He was angry. So much so that His anger burned hot (v. 11 ESV). But Moses asked the Lord to spare the people, and the Lord did.

Soon after, the Lord gives one of the most important statements about His character. The Lord said, "The LORD—the LORD is a compassionate and gracious God, slow to anger and abounding in faithful love and truth" (34:6). The Lord does have anger. But His anger is righteous. And even then, He is slow to manifest it. We see this in the life of Ahab.

The Lord was angry with Ahab and his people. The Lord sent a famine that lasted three years. The people knew the famine was the judgment of God, and at any time they could have turned back to God and had the judgment removed. Instead, they went deeper into rebellion.

After Elijah humiliated the prophets of Baal and Asherah, Elijah did something hard to imagine:

> Then the LORD's fire fell and consumed the burnt offering, the wood, the stones, and the dust, and it licked up the water that was in the trench. When all the people saw it, they fell facedown and said, "The LORD, he is God! The LORD, he is God!"
>
> Then Elijah ordered them, "Seize the prophets of Baal! Do not let even one of them escape." So they seized them, and Elijah brought them down to the Wadi Kishon and slaughtered them there. (1 Kings 18:38–40)

Elijah gathered up the false prophets, took them to the river, and slaughtered them there. It was a clear expression of the slow, but very real, anger of God.

We, however, have to see that anger in light of Exodus 34:6. Right before the prophets were slaughtered, the people repented. God was about to send rain. God was about to restore blessing. The false prophets had an opportunity to repent, but they refused. God was slow to anger. He continually held back His righteous anger to give the people time to repent. Not just in that moment, but in the three years prior to this.

The three years of famine were certainly the judgment of God, but it was also the patient call of God for them to repent. Even the fire from heaven in front of the people was an opportunity to see the Lord and respond to Him. Over and over again, when the Lord had every right to destroy the people, He gave them opportunity after opportunity to respond.

Why? He is slow to anger.

When it says that God is "slow to anger" (Exod. 34:6), it means He has a long fuse. It is the very opposite of having a quick temper. His anger is always slow, it is always under control, it is always just, and it is always filled with moral goodness. His anger only attacks what is truly evil. Yet the wrath of God is real. God can burn with anger.[2]

We often struggle with moments in the Bible like Joshua 6, where the people of God destroy the entire nation of Jericho. It feels like an injustice. It seems unloving. But we forget that for seven days the Lord has the people march around the town carrying the mercy seat, giving the people a chance to respond. And on the last day, He gives them seven chances. The Lord is slow to anger and abounding in steadfast love.

Those who think of God as primarily angry have never read the Old Testament. Starting in the garden of Eden, the entire Old Testament is a study in the slowness of God's anger. There are thousands of times when God could have demonstrated just and righteous anger, but instead, He shows patience and steadfast love.

The overwhelming emphasis of the Old Testament is that God is patient, merciful, kind, and gracious before He is angry. I can't imagine any parent putting up with more grumbling, whining, and complaining than the Lord did from His people as they wandered in the wilderness.

As David Powlison reminds us: "God is slow to anger and full of undeserved kindness. He is like a parent who hangs in there, persistently loving a wayward child. He gets angry—really angry—at true evils. He shows further, spectacular kindness to people willing to deal with what's wrong."[3] That is the God of the Old Testament, as well as the God of the New Testament.

The Anger of Jesus

Jesus is God in the flesh. To behold Jesus is to behold God. He is the exact imprint of God (John 1:1–14; Col. 1:15; Heb. 1:3). When we wonder about the real character of God, we look to Jesus. This means, what we have been seeing about God throughout the Old Testament, we should also see when we look at Jesus. And we do.

Jesus got angry. One Sabbath day, Jesus entered a synagogue and saw a man with a withered hand. The Pharisees stood and watched to see if Jesus would heal him so they could accuse Him of breaking one of their man-made laws. Jesus asked them if it was lawful to do good and save a life on the Sabbath. They said nothing. Then Mark tells us, "After looking around at them with anger, he was grieved at the hardness of their hearts and told the man, 'Stretch out your hand'" (Mark 3:5a).

When Jesus walked into the temple and saw the people being exploited and His Father being rejected, He went away and carefully crafted a whip that He used to drive the money changers out (John 2:14–17). It was not an outburst of anger, but it was still anger.

Jesus was angry when His disciples rebuked parents for bringing their children to Him (Mark 10:14–16). And He often got angry at the self-righteousness, hypocrisy, and hard-heartedness of the religious leaders (Matt. 23:25–32).

But the most important example of the anger of Jesus is found in John 11, when He stood by the tomb of Lazarus and wept. When Jesus saw Mary and the others crying, it says that He was "deeply moved in his spirit and troubled" (v. 33). The words for "deeply moved" could more accurately be translated as *indignant* or *angry*. He was angry over the devastating realities of a fallen world, the consequences of sin, the reality of death, and the depth of unbelief. Jesus did not just weep over Lazarus. He knew what He was about to do for Lazarus. He wept with a heart filled with anger over the effect of sin on a world He loves.[4]

Jesus got angry. But not very often. He was slow to anger and was abounding in steadfast love and faithfulness. That is truly remarkable.

When you consider the amount of injustice Jesus experienced toward Himself, and the injustice He saw against those He loved, it's amazing that we do not see more anger from Him. He was never angry toward those who sought to stone Him, arrest Him, and make plans to kill Him. When reviled, He did not open His mouth (1 Pet. 2:23). While hanging on the cross, being mocked, He cried, "Father, forgive them, for they know not what they do" (Luke 23:34 ESV). There was Jesus, a man who knew no sin, being killed like a common criminal, yet there was no anger in Him toward those who treated Him unjustly.

Jesus never got angry over any injustice toward Himself. Even when His enemies continued to reject Him and made plans to kill Him, He kept inviting them to believe and longed for them to be spared from the wrath of God (John 10:34–39).

In all of the accounts of Jesus, there seem to be only five specific times when He was angry. It took so much to stir up His anger. He could have been angry all the time, but instead, He was rarely angry. And His anger was never about the injustice done toward Him, but the injustice done toward others. His anger was reserved for sin, death, injustice, exploitation of people, and hypocrisy.

The anger of Jesus is always rooted in His love for people. The intensity of His anger flows from the intensity of His love. As the perfect picture of the love of God, He must defend the weak, helpless, and victimized. It would be unloving for those things not to make Him angry. His anger is good, loving, righteous, and necessary. Like His Father, He is slow to anger but gets angry when love demands it.

Be Angry!

Since we were created in the image of God (Gen. 1:27) and re-created to be conformed into the image of Christ (2 Cor. 5:17), then we are most like our true selves when we are most like God. The work of Christ on the cross, in absorbing the just wrath of God for our sins and being raised victorious over sin, means that by the power of the Spirit, we might be like Jesus and should strive to be like Jesus (Rom. 8:29; 12:1–3). The character of Christ is not just a model for us; it is a mandate.

Maybe that truth gets to the heart of the strange command by the apostle Paul in Ephesians 4:26a when he says, "Be angry and do not sin." Let's be clear: This verse is a command. We are commanded to "be angry." We are also commanded to "not sin" in our anger. This means that there is a type of anger that is righteous and holy, a type of anger that is not sinful. There is a type of anger that was modeled by the One who knew no sin (2 Cor. 5:21), yet could be angry. God has placed in our hearts the capacity for a type of anger that is not only good but necessary—and commanded.

When Paul commanded the church to get angry, he was doing so in the context of calling them to no longer walk in their old way of life. They were calloused, hard-hearted, living in sensuality, greed, and impurity, but they were not to act like that anymore. Now that they had come to Christ, they were to "put off" all of those things (Eph. 4:22 ESV).

In that context, Paul told them to get angry. Angry over what? Angry over sin. Angry over indifference to sin. Angry over the years that sin stole from them. The pain, suffering, conflict, shame, and bondage that sin led them into. They must not stay morally indifferent about sin. Sin needs to make them angry; not angry over everyone else's sin, but angry over their own.

About this passage, Martyn Lloyd-Jones said:

> You have to get right away from the world's sins; you have got to learn to be angry about them; you must be roused; you must not be complacent and say that sin does not matter! Such an attitude belongs to their past, he said, but they must not be like that any longer. A failure to react with indignation and anger against sin and evil is always a sign of moral decadence and of godlessness and of irreligion. . . . Our Lord was angry when he observed manifestations of sin. And what measures our approximations to him is that we manifest a similar

> reaction when confronted by similar things. It is our duty to be angry at certain points and with respect to certain matters.[5]

In other words, our closeness to Christ is manifested by whether we hate what Jesus hates. We cannot be indifferent toward those things Jesus loved, nor can we be indifferent toward the things Jesus hated. If it angers Jesus, it must anger us. When we do not love what God loves, that is sin. And when we do not hate what God hates, that, too, is sin.

The question is not: "Do we get angry?" We all get angry. The question is: "Do we only get angry over what makes Jesus angry?"

Do the things that angered Jesus anger you?

Righteous Anger

The man for the day must possess righteous anger. What stirs up his passion to be the man for the day is hatred for sin and injustice. But he must only be angry in a way that reflects the heart and love of Jesus. Our anger must be slow, always under control, always just, and always filled with moral goodness. Our anger must be reserved for that which makes God angry.

The man for the day must have righteous anger, but he must be careful with this anger. When talking about righteous anger in our day, John Piper wisely said:

> The present state of my mind, both biblically and culturally on this question about anger, is that anger is a dangerous emotion—not necessarily sinful. God, by the way, is the only person who is holy enough to manage it really well. And he does get angry, and he never sins. But we, however, being fallen and sinful, must consider it much more dangerous for us than it is for God. It's not dangerous for God. Nothing is dangerous for God. It has a proper place, therefore, only when it comes slowly, leaves quickly, and in between, is truly governed by a love for people and the glory of God.[6]

Any outburst of anger is a sin. Any anger that does not flow from love is a sin. Any anger that does not have at its core a zeal for the name and glory of Christ is a sin. Any anger that does not promote the good of others is a sin. Any anger that tears down the weak instead of upholding the weak is sin. And sinful anger must make us angry!

The man for the day must always be angry over his own sin, more than the sin of others. What angers us is not the speck in someone else's eye, but the plank in our own (Matt. 7:3–5). We must hate our sin. We must wage war on our sin. We must see the way our sin affects us and all those around us, and hate it as much as God does.

I am convinced that if there is a problem in my home, the first place I must look is myself. I must take responsibility first before putting the responsibility on others. I must be the first to examine myself and the first to repent.

The man for the day must be angry over the injustices of his day. In our day, we must be angry over abortion. The exploitation of women and children through pornography must fill us with the righteous anger of God. We must be angry over anything that takes advantage of women or hurts children. We must be angry over any form of ethnic or racial prejudice. We must be angry over anything that profanes the name of God or mocks Jesus Christ. We must be angry over the feminist agenda that undermines biblical manhood and womanhood and hurts women and little girls.

In Psalm 119:53, David, a man after God's own heart (1 Sam. 13:14; Acts 13:22), said, "Hot indignation seizes me because of the wicked, who forsake your law" (ESV).

I am deeply bothered by a generation of unbothered men; men who are not deeply bothered by the wickedness, injustice, and spiritual lostness around the world. I am concerned about a generation of men who do not abhor sin the way God does and are not angered by the aggressive attack of the Enemy on women and children. Where are the men angry over pornography and its effects on our culture?

History has recorded that more than 80 percent of Nazi recruits came from the Protestant church of Germany. This means, that as Hitler systematically killed six million Jews, the church of the day not only watched it but actively participated in it. The church should have been angry, but they were not. They failed to possess the anger of God.

While unrighteous anger does not produce the righteousness of God, righteous anger does (James 1:19–20). Any anger that does not produce righteousness, is not righteous anger. Righteousness is always the fruit of righteous anger. That is why it's called righteous anger. When God is angry, His motives are always right, and His goal is always righteousness. It is always for the good of others and the glory of God. And the men of the day must have it.

The Man for the Day

The man for the day wages war on sinful anger. He knows that his anger undermines every good work God wants to do in him and in others. He knows that anger does not produce righteousness.

The man for the day understands the anger of God. He knows that God is slow to anger and abounding in steadfast love. He does not get angry over injustices done to him. He makes sure that any anger he feels is the righteous anger of God.

The man for the day hates what God hates. He is not morally indifferent. He is not unbothered by what bothers God. He hates his sin and does all he can to kill it. Starting with his own. He hates wickedness and injustice, and he stands against it. The man for the day has the affections of Christ.

Be the man for the day!

Chapter 9

Prayer

Prayer: Working with God to accomplish His purposes in and through you.

AS A PASTOR, I have sat by the bedside of many dying men. But this was different. I was sitting next to a man I loved and admired. He was a man who had been a model for me in ministry. He was in his last days, and I had come to his house in hopes of hearing as much as I could from him before he died. What I didn't expect was to hear a story that shocked me and broke my heart, a story I honestly wish I hadn't heard.

This man told me about being in college in the late 1950s, when he received a call telling him that he needed to come home as quickly as possible. His mother, who had undergone a rather routine surgery, was not doing well. As soon as he heard, he got in the car and drove as fast as he could the 250 miles from Arkansas to Texas.

He stopped to tell me how much he loved his mother. There were many family circumstances that made him spend a lot of time worrying about her. He had always looked out for her when it seemed no one else did. Because of this, they were particularly close.

He told me that, as he drove, all he did was pray. He prayed that he would get there in time to see her. He prayed for her complete recovery. He just prayed, and prayed, and prayed.

He arrived at the hospital, parked his car, and made his way to her room. When he got to her room, all he saw was a cleaning crew, changing the sheets and mopping the floor. His mother had died and had been removed from the room.

My heart broke as I heard that story; I couldn't imagine his pain. But what he told me next broke my heart even more. It would have been hard to hear this from anyone, but even more so from an eighty-year-old man who had spent his life in the ministry and was a hero in the faith to me. He said, "From that moment on, I never really prayed again."

I had heard this man make jokes in sermons about how much his wife prayed, and how if he needed something he just asked her to pray about it. People laughed. They assumed he was kidding. But he wasn't. He didn't pray. His hurt, anger, and resentment toward God for not answering his prayer the way he wanted caused him to grow cynical. And cynical people don't pray.

To be effective in prayer, we must come to God with a childlike faith. A cynical spirit is the opposite of childlike faith. Cynicism questions the goodness of God and makes it impossible to move closer toward our heavenly Father.[1] The foundation for prayer is our confidence in the goodness of the Father (Luke 11:1–13).

We must also understand the purpose of prayer as more than just receiving what we ask for. Prayer is the language by which we cultivate an intimate relationship with God. Prayer is how we speak to God and how God speaks to us. Prayer is the way we partner with God to accomplish His purposes in and through us.

This man had lost his confidence in God and in prayer. Cynicism took its place. And he spent the last sixty years of his life like many of us are spending ours—prayerless.

The Missing Piece

It's a sad statement, but I'm afraid it's a true statement: Most men don't pray. Some of it may be cynicism. Some of it may be a misunderstanding of prayer. Some of it is just being in a church context in which no one really prays—including the pastor. I'm sure some of it is a lack of teaching and training. And a lot of it is spiritual apathy. Whatever the reason, most men don't pray. At least not enough to really accomplish anything.

I get invited to a lot of men's retreats, men's banquets, men's events, men's breakfasts, and men's dinners, but I have never been invited to a men's prayer meeting. At least one that actually spent time praying. It could be because men's prayer meetings don't have special guests, or it could be that there just aren't many men's prayer meetings. That could be because pastors know men won't show up. And I think that's because, much like the cynical man who never prays, we aren't really sure it does anything.

Steve Gaines, who has been a personal role model to me in the area of prayer, said:

> When I read the book of Acts, I am embarrassed. Why does our brand of Christianity look so insipid compared to the believers of the first century? Where has the power gone? Has God changed, or have we? . . . Our lack of spiritual power in Christianity today is not due to the sermons we preach or the songs we sing. Rather, it is due to our lack of prayer. We do not pray like it matters.[2]

We have come a long way from the 120 men and women in the upper room who prayed for forty days until the power of God fell on them (Acts 1). They knew they could not accomplish anything for God without the power of God, and that they could not receive the power of God without prayer.

It seems that most men have come to believe that prayer is no longer the essential ingredient for being used by God. We may not say that verbally, but we say it by our lack of prayer. And that's a shame, not only because of how badly this generation needs the power of God, but because prayer is one of the primary means by which God fulfills His purposes in and through you. If any man wants to be the man for the day, he must be a man of prayer.

What God Wants

The pastoral epistles, 1–2 Timothy and Titus, are not written about men. They are written about the local church. But each of them is written from one godly man to another godly man, pleading with them to raise up godly men (1 Tim. 3:1–7; 2 Tim. 2:2; Titus 1:5). For this reason, these letters are uniquely important for men.

In Paul's first letter to Timothy, he writes: "I desire then that in every place the men should pray" (1 Tim. 2:8a ESV). I find this so interesting. He does not say that he wants all the men in all the churches to lead, or teach, or disciple, or even witness. He says he wants all the men in every place to pray.

I'm convicted by this. Honestly, if I was asked to write a letter to a church and give one piece of instruction to the men, I'm not sure I would say, "Just have them pray." Given the lack of prayer gatherings for men, I'm not sure many would say that prayer should be the priority for men. But that's what Paul said, and it's what God wants. God wants men to pray. But why?

Maybe because God does not use methods, he uses men. *Praying* men. E. M. Bounds says it this way:

> Men are God's method. The world is looking for better methods; God is looking for better men. . . . What the church needs today is not more machinery or better, not new organizations or more novel methods, but men whom the Holy Spirit can use—men of prayer, men mighty in prayer. The

> Holy Spirit does not flow through methods, but through men. He does not come on machinery, but on men. He does not anoint plans, but men—men of prayer.[3]

The man for the day is a man who is ready and willing to be used by God in whatever way God chooses. It is a man who knows that God is looking for men to use, and he wants to be that man. We want to be the men God chooses to advance His kingdom all around us. But it is impossible to be that man without prayer. Impossible.

Why is it impossible for God to use a prayerless man? Because prayer is the primary weapon that God uses to advance His kingdom in and through His people. John Piper says this so well:

> *We cannot know what prayer is for until we know that life is war.* Life is war. That's not all it is. But it is always that. Our weakness in prayer is owing largely to our neglect of this truth. Prayer is primarily a wartime walkie-talkie for the mission of the church as it advances against the powers of darkness and unbelief. It is not surprising that prayer malfunctions when we try to make it a domestic intercom to call upstairs for more comforts in the den. God has given prayer as a wartime walkie-talkie so that we can call headquarters for everything we need as the kingdom of Christ advances in the world. Prayer gives *us* the

> significance of frontline forces and gives *God* the glory of a limitless Provider. The one who gives the power gets the glory. Thus, prayer safeguards the supremacy of God in missions while linking us with endless grace for every need.[4]

Maybe that is a part of the underlying cynicism. It's not that we don't know we *should* pray, it's that we don't know we *must* pray. We don't really believe that the desire to be used of God must be accompanied by prayer. And this is where Elijah is so helpful.

The Sound of Rain

After Elijah called down fire from heaven and slaughtered the false prophets, he turned to King Ahab and gave him instructions on what to do next. Elijah said to Ahab, "Go up, eat and drink, for there is the sound of a rainstorm" (1 Kings 18:41). Now remember, up until this point, the entire story of Elijah has revolved around rain.

God was withholding rain as a sign of His judgment on their sin (17:1). As a result, there was a severe famine (v. 12). After three years, the Lord commanded Elijah to find Ahab and tell him it was going to rain (18:1–2). His meeting with Ahab is what led to the showdown on Mount Carmel, but still, there was no rain.

But when that battle was over, in response to the clear promise of God, Elijah told Ahab it was about to rain. The only problem was, when he said this, there was not one cloud in the sky. No sign of rain whatsoever. No meteorology report or rain clouds, just a promise from God. So when Ahab went away to get something to eat, Elijah went to the top of the mountain to pray. He was praying for God to bring the rain that He had promised; the rain Elijah said was about to come.

Elijah bowed down with his face between his knees. He begged the Lord for rain. He sent his servant to go and look toward the sea to see if there were any clouds. Nothing. He prayed again. His servant looked again. Nothing. He prayed again. His servant looked again. Nothing. Seven times this happens.

After the seventh time, his servant said, "Behold, a cloud as small as a man's hand is coming up from the sea." Elijah replied, "Go up, say to Ahab, 'Prepare your chariot and go down, so that the heavy shower does not stop you'" (v. 44 NASB1995). And in that moment, the sky grew dark with clouds and the rain began to pour down.

My leadership style is often "Ready. Fire. Aim." Meaning, I say we are going to do something before we even know how we are going to do it. Sometimes it works out. Sometimes it fails spectacularly. But this is not what Elijah was doing. Elijah had a promise from God. God said it would rain. Elijah believed the promise and prayed until God fulfilled the promise. And God did.

A Man Like Us

Elijah was an Old Testament prophet of God. He was called and anointed to receive a word from God and speak a word from God. He was given a prophet's ear and a prophet's mouth. God gave him a specific word for a specific time, and the word he spoke was the word of God. He was a mediator between God and man. But in many ways, he even seems to rise above many of the other prophets. His life was incredible.

Elijah stopped the rain, multiplied oil, raised a boy from the dead, called down fire from heaven, slaughtered prophets, brought the rain back, outran the king's chariot on foot, and was taken to heaven in a chariot of fire. In many ways, his life is unparalleled in the Old Testament.

Not that God is unable to do all those things again, but we must ask ourselves: Is Elijah, as an Old Testament prophet, really someone we can emulate? Is his life reproducible at all? To be honest, in many ways, the answer is no. For one primary reason: We are not Old Testament prophets.

Yet, just when we think that his power, effectiveness, and work is beyond anything we could accomplish, we get a glimmer of hope. One little passage in James 5 helps us to see that Elijah was not just the man for his day; he is a model for us to be the men for our day.

James says, "The effective prayer of a righteous man can accomplish much. Elijah was a man with a nature like ours, and he prayed earnestly that it would not rain, and it did not rain on the earth for three years and six months. Then he prayed again, and the sky poured rain and the earth produced its fruit" (James 5:16b–18 NASB1995).

"Elijah was a man with a nature like ours." That's an important statement. James says it to motivate us to pray. He wants us to see that the primary secret to Elijah's life was not much of a secret. It was the power of God through prayer. Elijah was just a man. A man like us.

How did Elijah call down the rain? He prayed. James says that the one part of Elijah's life that we should absolutely emulate is his prayer life. His prayer life was the secret to his life. His life, from beginning to end, modeled the power of a praying man. And since Elijah was a man just like us, that power is still available to the men who want it.

The simple principle James teaches us about prayer from the life of Elijah is this: Effective prayers prayed by righteous men accomplish something. God's work in us and through us is accomplished by prayer.

Effective Prayer

If the "effective prayer" of a righteous man accomplishes much (James 5:16 NASB1995), what is effective prayer? The word *effective* there means "energized" or "working." It could mean "the kind of prayer that is energized by God" or "the kind of prayer that works with power."[5] There is a kind of prayer that seems to be effective, prayer that is energized by God. It's the kind of prayers Elijah prayed. When we look back to 1 Kings 18, we see four marks of "effective prayer" (v. 44 NASB1995).

First, effective prayer is biblical. Effective prayer is based on a promise of God. Elijah prays what God had already promised. It used to bother me when people would pray back to God what God already said. I thought if God already knows it, He doesn't need us to remind Him. But the reality is that effective prayer always starts with the Word of God. It is motivated by a promise of God. The promises of God are fuel for our prayer.

I have discovered that the seasons in which I struggle with prayer are the seasons when I am not saturated with the Word of God. George Müller, who recorded more than fifty thousand specific prayers during his life and ministry, found that the secret to his prayer life was starting the day with God's Word before prayer. He found that he was led naturally into great prayer when his soul was first fed with the Word of God.[6]

Effective prayer always starts first with God's Word. It is motivated, informed, and fueled by what God has already said. When we pray according to God's Word, we know He hears and answers our prayers (1 John 5:14).

Second, effective prayer is fervent. James 5:17 says that Elijah "prayed earnestly." And he did. When he got on his knees and put his face to the ground, he was communicating through his posture how desperately he needed the Lord (1 Kings 18:42). He was pleading with the Lord to fulfill His promise. Elijah prayed like it mattered. He prayed like God would hear him. He prayed like his prayers would change something. And they did!

Jesus sweat drops of blood when He prayed (Luke 22:44). Jacob wrestled with God all night (Gen. 32:24–32). Hannah prayed so fervently that Samuel thought she was drunk (1 Sam. 1:13–14). David longed, pleaded, and begged for the Lord to answer his prayers (2 Sam. 12:16; Ps. 17).

When is the last time you prayed like that? When is the last time you prayed like prayer mattered? How often do you plead with God for something specific? Effective prayer is fervent prayer.

Third, effective prayer is expectant. Elijah prayed and sent his servant to look for clouds. Seven times he asked his servant to go and look. He knew they would come eventually. He wasn't sure when or how, but he knew they would come. Elijah expected God to work.

What do you want God to do for you? Do you have any lists? Anything specific? How will you ever know if God answers your prayers if you have no specific prayers? Vague prayers do not get specific answers.

David said, "In the morning, Lord, you hear my voice; in the morning I plead my case to you and watch expectantly" (Ps. 5:3). I love that verse. Pray a specific prayer in the morning and then watch expectantly for how the Lord will work.

Prayer is not expecting that the Lord will answer every prayer the way I pray it, but it is expecting that God will answer my prayers. When we communicate with God out of a desire to cultivate intimacy with Him and a desire to see His kingdom advanced in us and through us, we can expect that God will work through those prayers.

When Andrea and I got married, we made a list of twelve specific things we needed the Lord to do in our life. I remember how much fun it was to keep praying and keep watching. In many unexpected ways, in His own time, with His perfect wisdom, the Lord answered. The Lord wants us to pray with confident expectation that He will answer in the way that is best.

Finally, effective prayer is persistent. After Elijah prayed for rain six times, there was not one cloud in the sky. Not one. And yet he kept praying.

I'm deeply convicted by this point. I feel confident that if I was in Elijah's situation, after the first time I would have just assumed that God didn't care, that He had totally forgotten me, and there was no use in praying anymore. Pitiful, I know! We are so quick to stop praying. So quick to think God is not listening. So impatient.

Effective prayer keeps at it. Effective prayer keeps asking. Effective prayer knows that, for some reason, God responds to persistence. Just like in the story of the friend who knocks on the door at midnight looking for something to eat (Luke 11). Jesus tells this story of a persistent friend to make a point about prayer. The Lord then says, "I tell you, even though he won't get up and give him anything because he is his friend, yet because of his friend's shameless boldness, he will get up and give him as much as he needs. So I say to you, ask, and it will be given to you. Seek, and you will find. Knock, and the door will be opened to you" (vv. 8–9).

Effective prayer is biblical, fervent, expectant, and persistent. That's the kind of prayer that brings down the fire from heaven. Not to consume an altar, but to consume our hearts. Our desire for the real, felt, experienced, manifest presence of God in our life comes through this kind of prayer. When we pray like this, we learn that our prayers matter.

A Righteous Man

James tells us that the kind of prayer that accomplishes something is effective prayer, prayed by a righteous man (James 5:16). This means the effectiveness of prayer, to some degree, is determined by the holiness of the person praying.

When we talk about righteousness, we talk about both positional and practical righteousness. Positional righteousness refers to a right standing with God that only comes by grace and through faith in the work of Christ on our behalf. This is what Paul is referring to when he says, "He made the one who did not know sin to be sin for us, so that in him we might become the righteousness of God" (2 Cor. 5:21). We are declared right with God through the sacrifice of Christ (Rom. 5:1–11). As a result, there is no condemnation for those who have trusted Christ (8:1). They are positionally righteous, not because of any work of their own, but by the work of Christ alone (Eph. 2:1–10).

But when we talk about righteousness, we must also talk about practical righteousness. When we trust in Christ alone for the forgiveness of our sins, are justified by grace, and declared right with God, we spend the rest of our lives becoming practically what we already are positionally.

This is why Hebrews 12:14 says we should pursue holiness, without which no one will see the Lord. This is why we discipline ourselves for godliness (1 Tim. 4:7–8). This is why we apply great effort to walk with God and remain pure before him (Phil. 2:12; Eph. 4:17–24).

One of the most important promises in my entire life is, "Blessed are the pure in heart, for they shall see God" (Matt. 5:8 ESV). Few things motivate me to purity more than my desire to see God. I want to know Him, experience Him, be intimate with Him, and receive everything He has for me. Without purity, I will miss out on those things. Those who are used by God are clean vessels (2 Tim. 2:21 ESV).

The one who wants to ascend the hill of the Lord, enjoy His presence, and hear from Him, must walk with clean hands and a pure heart (Ps. 24:4). David says that if we hide sin in our hearts, the Lord will not hear us (66:18).

Our prayers are affected by our purity. We cannot continually grieve the Holy Spirit of God and quench the fire of God and expect for our prayers to be effective. Elijah's effectiveness in prayer flowed out of his life of purity. And so does ours.

Once we are positionally righteous, in a right standing with God through faith in Christ, we can be confident that we have access to God through our mediator Jesus Christ (1 Tim. 2:5). Even when we don't know what to pray, Jesus hears the cries of our hearts and brings our prayer to the Father who loves us and longs to give us good gifts (Matt. 7:11). This is incredibly good news.

Yet the Bible is also clear that the power of God in our lives, the flow of His Spirit into us, the flow of His Spirit through us, our effectiveness in evangelism, the anointing of God on our lives, our ability to love and serve our family well, and the effectiveness of our prayers are all determined in some way by our pursuit of holiness every day. First Peter 3:12 says, "The eyes of the Lord are on the righteous and his ears are open to their prayer. But the face of the Lord is against those who do what is evil." A pure heart can only make our prayers more effective and more powerful.

Lord, Teach Us to Pray

I want to be as honest with you as I can. Over the course of my Christian life, there has been no area of spiritual growth that has consistently made me feel more defeated than the area of prayer. Maybe it's the way I'm wired. Maybe it's because it's easier for me to move than to sit. But I think the primary reason for the struggle is the way in which God wants to use my life.

Maybe I have struggled through prayer in order to encourage the men God has called me to encourage. I am confident most men struggle with prayer. Most men want to pray; they just find it incredibly difficult.

In Luke 11, I believe Jesus's disciples felt the same thing. They had seen Jesus pray and wanted to learn to pray like Him. So, they asked Him, "Lord, teach us to pray" (v. 1). One of the most encouraging things I've heard about prayer is this: "God wants to teach you to pray more than you want to learn to pray."[7] So, ask Him to teach you. He will.

Read Luke 11. See God's desire to teach you to pray. See His desire to answer prayers. See the love of the Father who longs to give good gifts to His children. Learn to pray through the pattern of the Lord's Prayer. Most of all, just start praying. Not just to get things from Him, but to cultivate intimacy with Him. And not just to get Him to do something through you, but to do something in you. Believe that the effective prayer of a righteous man does, in fact, accomplish much!

The Man for the Day

The man for the day despises cynicism (Prov. 1:22). He knows that it flows from arrogance and a lack of faith. He knows that cynicism always hinders the power, presence, and purposes of God. He is not cynical. He is filled with faith, confidence, and hope in God.

The man for the day is honest about his prayer life. If he struggles to pray, he admits it. He acknowledges it to God and others. He asks the Lord to help him pray. Over and over again. He believes that God wants him to be a praying man, and he will not rest until he is.

The man for the day leads his wife and family in prayer. He humbles himself, and even when it's awkward, prays with his wife and kids. He also prays for his wife and kids.

The man for the day believes his prayers matter. He knows there are things God will only do through prayer. So he seeks to live a morally pure life so that his prayers are effective.

Be the man for the day!

Chapter 10

Weakness

Weakness: Finding strength through embracing the depth of your neediness.

AFTER SIX HUNDRED hours of chemo, twenty-six rounds of radiation, four spinal taps to get chemo to her brain, and one major surgery, Andrea was declared cancer free. We had watched another young woman, diagnosed at the same time with the same cancer, slowly and painfully drift into eternity. This made us even more aware of how humbled and grateful we should be for Andrea's healing. She is a miracle.

Day by day, as Andrea was regaining her strength, something strange was happening to me. I was growing more and more weak. Over the course of the next few months I lost thirty pounds and struggled daily with debilitating and chronic nausea. I had no idea that this was the beginning of the most difficult years of my life.

That story is enough for another book, but the reality is, I was physically, emotionally, and spiritually exhausted. The weight I had been carrying had begun to manifest itself in physical symptoms, and I could not seem to get it under control. A year after Andrea finished treatment, I was in the darkest place of my life and wanted nothing more than to leave the ministry.

Through the following two years, by the grace and promises of God and the company of good friends, the Lord began to restore my strength—and my joy. Day by day, moment by moment, the Lord proved Himself faithful. When I wanted to give up, the Lord would not let me. He who had shown me many troubles and calamities, revived me again (Ps. 71:20).

It was in those years—the most difficult years of my life—that the Lord gave me great encouragement through a man who found himself in a similar place. He was a man of incredible strength, who found himself in a place of incredible weakness. And in this man, I saw a picture of myself. Not in his strength, but in his weakness.

The Wilderness of Spiritual Depression

The life and ministry of Elijah, recorded in 1 Kings 17 and 18, is astonishing. His surrender, courage, resolve, power, and faith were unmatched. The Lord had raised him up and used him greatly. He stood in the face of kings, called the people to revival, and saw the nation repent by calling fire from heaven. He was the man for the day! And that is what makes the next moments of his life so surprising.

When Ahab went home and told Jezebel that Elijah had slaughtered all of her false prophets, she was furious. She immediately sent a message to Elijah, saying, "May the gods punish me and do so severely if I don't make your life like the life of one of them by this time tomorrow!" (19:2).

Jezebel was determined to kill Elijah. Determined to do it in the next twenty-four hours. But this is Elijah—the man who had just gone to battle against 450 false prophets in the presence of the entire nation, called down fire from heaven, slaughtered the prophets, and outran Ahab's chariot. If he wasn't fazed by that, why would he be fazed by the threats of Jezebel?

The next verse says, "Then Elijah became afraid and immediately ran for his life. When he came to Beer-sheba that belonged to Judah, he left his servant there" (v. 3). Beer-sheba is the farthest southern point of Judah. To say he ran from Jezreel to Beer-sheba is to say, "Elijah ran as far away as he possibly could." But that didn't seem far enough.

Elijah left his servant in Beer-sheba, and went another day's journey deep into the wilderness. When he was there, he sat under a tree and asked to die. The only prayer he had the strength to pray was, "I have had enough! LORD, take my life, for I'm no better than my ancestors" (v. 4). Translation: I can't do this anymore, I'm an idiot, I'm never going to amount to anything, and I just want to die.

I have five children. This kind of drama is not new to me. But this is not a five-year-old who didn't get his way—this is *Elijah*! He wasn't scared of anything! He had just slaughtered false prophets! Why was he so terrified? Why did he run so far away? Why was he praying to die?

I often say that Elijah is my favorite prophet. I resonate with him. I feel like we have a lot of similarities. Sure, I've never called down fire from heaven or slaughtered false prophets, but I have sat under a tree and thought I was worthless. I don't resonate with his strengths; I resonate with his weaknesses. It is in this place—hiding in the wilderness, sitting under a tree, completely exhausted—that I find a man who resonates with me deeply. I've been there. In some ways, all of us have.

As I have said before, I am convinced most men feel deeply ashamed, afraid, and inadequate. You may not struggle in the same way that Elijah did, but we all run away and hide from certain things. We all avoid certain things because of fear. We all struggle with deep areas of defeat, fear, weakness, and insecurity.

Up until this point, Elijah seemed fearless and invincible. But his short prayer exposed unseen things going on in his heart. He struggled with misplaced fears, misplaced strength, misplaced hope, and a misplaced identity. Deep inside this strong prophet was a weak, insecure, and hurting man. And we should find great comfort in this, because even though we may not pray the prayer that Elijah prayed, we can often feel the way Elijah felt.

In a moment, Elijah had gone from the mountain of manifest presence to the wilderness of spiritual depression. He had gone from this highest of highs to the lowest of lows. And since we all seem to take that same journey at times, the first question is: "How did he get there?"

Into the Wilderness

In the midst of all that Elijah remembered, there seem to be a few things he had forgotten. And those things he forgot seem to be the things that led him so far into the wilderness of spiritual depression. They are the things we all tend to forget.

He forgot his humanity. Wayne Cordeiro begins his wonderful book *Leading on Empty* by saying, "We don't forget that we are Christians. We forget that we are human, and that one oversight alone can debilitate the potential of our future."[1] He's right.

What was the most obvious reason for this moment in Elijah's life? He was exhausted. He was physically, emotionally, and spiritually exhausted. Surely, it wasn't that simple.

In a sense, it isn't that simple. Elijah had a lot of things going on. His prayer revealed the depth of his hidden fears, insecurities, and lack of identity. But it seems the first issue was his own exhaustion. He had forgotten he was human. How do we know this? We know it by the response of the Lord.

The Lord does not initially respond to Elijah's prayer with a lecture, correction, or even a Bible promise. The Lord answers him with a nap and a hot meal.

Elijah laid down and went to sleep. The Lord sent an angel to wake him up and tell him to eat. When he did, the Lord had provided a hot cake baked on hot stones and a jar of water. Elijah ate, drank, and went back to sleep. The Lord woke him up a second time and told him the same thing. He woke up, ate, and drank.

The Lord's first response to Elijah's prayer was two naps and two hot meals. Why? Because after his massive spiritual battle at Mount Carmel, his slaughtering prophets, his pleading with God in prayer, and his outrunning Ahab's chariot, he was physically exhausted.

One of the most profound things the Lord has taught me over the years is the reason I so often feel exhausted is because I am. No deeper issues. Nothing to overthink. The reason I feel tired is because I am tired. At the end of Andrea's battle with cancer, navigating work and four children, I was physically, emotionally, and mentally depleted.

I know many men who don't work hard enough. I know some lazy gluttons who need to be constantly told to get to work. The book of Proverbs is clear: These kinds of men are a disgrace. There are very few things worse than a lazy man.

Yet many men are going at an unsustainable pace. There are external pressures like work, family, kids' activities, and travel ball that are constantly making us move. Then, there are the internal issues of pride, trying to impress others, love of money, and fear of man that often keep us overcommitted. We have left no place for the spiritual and physical rest that life with God demands.

I am pastoring a church filled with people who are so overcommitted that they have no balance in their lives. They won't be able to sustain the pace and continue to have a healthy body or soul. They are forgetting that they are human and must have time and space to let their bodies and souls rest. It's unsustainable and unhealthy.

Elijah not only forgot his humanity; he forgot his adversary. In all of the excitement generated by the fire coming down from heaven, we tend to forget that Elijah was right in the middle of a massive spiritual battle. Imagine the amount of demonic activity surrounding that moment.

Paul tells us that our struggle is not against flesh and blood, but against the invisible forces in the heavenly places (Eph. 6:12). Elijah's battle was not only with the unseen forces of darkness in the heavenly places, but with the very real seen forces of demonic false prophets. This was as big a spiritual battle as anywhere in Scripture. In many ways, Elijah was a man who had just come home from war.

When talking about the spiritual battle, Peter says, "Be sober-minded, be alert. Your adversary the devil is prowling around like a roaring lion, looking for anyone he can devour" (1 Pet. 5:8). We always have an Enemy, and he is always looking for a way to devour us.

When Elijah was most exhausted, the Enemy launched his greatest attack. In that one moment in which Elijah was the most tired, the Enemy was the most alert. The Enemy waged a brand-new attack on a man who was thinking the war was over. He knew Elijah's insecurities, his weaknesses. He knew where he was vulnerable. He knew exactly how tired he was. And in that moment, in his weakness, the Enemy won a battle and made Elijah run for his life.

This is how the Enemy works. He knows when we are weakest. He knows when we are tired. He knows when we don't want to fight anymore. We get tired, but he doesn't. So he waits, as he did with Jesus, for an opportune time to tempt us (Luke 4:13). And it's most often in those moments in which we put our guard down and lose a battle we would normally win. When we put our guard down, the Enemy wages war.

The problem is, we forget that in every moment there is an Enemy who wants to take us down and ruin our lives. He never relents. He never gives up. He never stops watching and waiting for our weakest moment. And if we forget this, like Elijah, we will find ourselves very quickly in a place we never intended to be.

Finally, Elijah forgot the depth of his dependency. Our first response to Elijah running away is, "Wait, this isn't Elijah! Who is this?" The answer: This is Elijah when he forgets his need for the Lord. And this is every man when we forget how much we need God, every moment of every day.

After Elijah's second nap and second meal, he went and hid in a cave. He felt unappreciated, discouraged, and alone. The Lord commanded him to get outside of the cave and stand on the mountain before the Lord.

The Lord passed by in a strong wind that tore the mountains and broke rocks into pieces, "but the LORD was not in the wind. After the wind there was an earthquake, but the LORD was not in the earthquake. After the earthquake there was a fire, but the LORD was not in the fire" (1 Kings 19:11b–12a).

And after the fire, there was the sound of a low whisper—a still, small voice. It was in that voice he heard the Lord giving him direction. It was in that moment that the Lord gave him specific instructions on what was next.

Elijah's entire life had been big, miraculous moments. He had been used to seeing God in the dramatic. But not now. Now, he would only be able to hear the Lord if he listened for the low whisper. And that is significant. And so gracious of the Lord.

The Lord knew that Elijah's body and soul needed to be restored, so the Lord chose to speak to him in a way that demanded he be still and quiet. It wasn't just about the end result of giving Elijah instruction; it was about the process of forcing him to stop, wait, be quiet, and rest until the word from God came.

This is such an important reminder for us. Psalm 23 makes it clear that our souls are restored as we lay beside still waters. Our souls are restored when we follow the leadership of the Lord to a quiet place to sit, breathe, read, and hear from God. God speaks to us in a still, small voice because it forces us to be still and quiet. He speaks to us in a still, small voice because it is the means by which He gets what He wants most from us: intimacy with Him.

In our moments of weakness, the Lord wants us to remember just how much we need Him. He wants to remind us that we are one moment away from making a mess of our entire lives. He wants us to be constantly aware that there is never a moment in which we don't desperately need Him.

The Way Out of the Wilderness

When the Lord invited Elijah out of the cave and spoke in a low whisper, He gave Elijah specific direction on what to do next. Elijah felt done with God, but God was not done with Elijah. God had something more for him. And step-by-step, the Lord restored him.

One of the things the Lord told him to do was go to Damascus, where he would not only anoint a new king over Syria and a new king over Israel, but he would anoint a new prophet, Elisha. Elisha would not only take Elijah's place after his death but would become a companion to him until that time.

There is so much hope and encouragement in the way the Lord dealt with Elijah during these moments. God was so patient and so kind. The Lord did not lecture him; He just led him. Like a good shepherd who knows when his sheep need to be led to still waters, the Lord led Elijah and restored him, just like He does with us.

I do not in any way want to oversimplify the moments of darkness in our lives. Trust me, I've been there. In my darkest moment the Lord revealed so many hard things to me. It was a season of deep healing from some deep hurts. The Lord showed me things I would have never seen if it wasn't for those seasons of weakness. This is not always a simple process.

But in the midst of all that, the things I needed the most were simple things that I had neglected. I needed rest. I needed food. I needed exercise. I needed to take care of my body.

I also needed to take care of my soul. I needed to sit, be still, and wait for the still, small voice of the Lord. I needed God to sustain me with a new promise, new hope, and new mercies. I needed to hear from God. We all need this. And our weaknesses remind us how much we need this.

I needed community. I needed close friends and companions who would ensure I didn't walk further into the wilderness, but back to the mountain. Like we often do, Elijah wanted to be alone and left his servant. But the Lord would not let him stay that way very long. The Lord led him to Elisha and the school of the prophets to remind him of his need for others.

But everything in us wants to neglect the things we need most. Like Elijah, we want to run away and hide. We don't want to see anyone or hear from anyone. We don't even want to hear from God. But the primary answer is to get back to the basic things we don't want: eating, sleeping, resting, hearing from God, and being in the company of believers.

I recently had the opportunity to speak to a large group of Christian schoolteachers at the end of the school year. I shared with them the surefire best way to feel energized and restored before the next school year. I assured them this was not just my best advice, but the biblical way of feeling refreshed and restored. I can summarize it in seven words: Sleep, eat, and get alone with God. That's how God restored Elijah's strength, and that is how God restores ours.

The Importance of Weakness

This moment in Elijah's life is such a gift to us. If we only knew Elijah in his miraculous moments, we would never know that he was a man like us. It's his weaknesses that make us resonate with him.

The reason for this is because behind every strong man is a weak man. Behind every façade of bravery, courage, strength, and invincibility is a scared, insecure, and hurting man. And at some point, just like He did with Elijah, the Lord will do something to expose that. He has to. If He doesn't, we can never truly be used by Him. Because maybe, just maybe, the secret to being used by God is not the external picture of strength, but the internal reality of weakness.

What the Lord taught Elijah in those moments of weakness were the most important lessons of his life. It was there, hiding in a cave, praying he would die, that the Lord brought him to a new place of surrender, humility, dependence, intimacy, and all the things more necessary to be used by God.

None of us want to have our weaknesses exposed. None of us want to be in places where we see who we really are. But it is in those places, and often only in those places, that the Lord develops the strength we need to be used by Him.

I began this book with a story of being terrified that God would put me through hard things if I surrendered to Him. And I was right! The more I surrendered, the harder things got. Yet, those seasons of my life that have been the hardest ended up being the most important. I spent so much time fearing those moments, all the while not realizing that the Lord will only make me the man He wants me to be through those moments I wanted to avoid.

God does not make a man through seasons of strength. God makes a man through seasons of weakness. Because it is only in our weakness that the Lord shows His strength.

In his wonderful book *Weakness Is the Way*, J. I. Packer says:

> Often linked with the sense of weakness—sometimes as cause, sometimes as effect—is the feeling of failure. . . . The truth, however, is that in many respects, and certainly in spiritual matters, we are all weak and inadequate, and we need to face it. Sin, which disrupts all relationships, has disabled us all across the board. We need to be aware of our limitations and to let this awareness work in us humility and self-distrust, and a realization of our helplessness on our own. Thus we may learn our need to depend on Christ, our Savior and Lord, at every turn of the road, to practice that dependency as one of the constant habits of our heart, and hereby to discover what Paul discovered before us: "when I am weak, then I am strong" (2 Cor. 12:10).[2]

As Packer says, weakness is the way. Could it be that the very things you want so badly to get rid of are the things God is using to remind you of how much you need Him? Could it be that those fears, insecurities, and feelings of inadequacy are the means by which God will make you strong?

If it wasn't for Elijah's wilderness moment, we might just leave this story impressed with Elijah. But because of his weakness, we leave this story impressed with the Lord. Elijah's secret was not ultimately his strength, power, or resolve. His secret was the presence of God.

And that's good news for us, because the same presence that was with him then, can be with us now. It's God who makes men for the day. And most often, He does it not through our strength, but through our weakness. The kind of weakness that drives us into His presence.

The Man for the Day

The man for the day is honest about his weaknesses. He openly acknowledges his fears, insecurities, and inadequacies. He knows his humanity and his need for rest.

The man for the day does not allow himself or his family to be overcommitted. He knows that in order for his body and soul to thrive, they need time and attention and space. He fights the pressure to be all things to all people.

The man for the day knows that life is war and lives life on alert. He knows that in his weakest moments, the Enemy is ready to strike. He sees the Enemy and does not give in.

The man for the day allows his weaknesses to drive him toward humility, intimacy, and dependency. He does not allow his weaknesses to drive him to despair and isolation. He knows that weakness is the way to what he needs most: the strength only the Lord can supply.

Be the man for the day!

Notes

Introduction

1. Charles Spurgeon, *The Metropolitan Tabernacle Pulpit*, Volume 34 (Pilgrim Publications, 1974), 73–84.

2. Spurgeon, *Metropolitan Tabernacle Pulpit*, 74.

3. Spurgeon, *Metropolitan Tabernacle Pulpit*, 78.

4. Spurgeon, *Metropolitan Tabernacle Pulpit*, 83.

5. Spurgeon, *Metropolitan Tabernacle Pulpit*, 84.

6. Spurgeon, *Metropolitan Tabernacle Pulpit*, 84.

7. Spurgeon, *Metropolitan Tabernacle Pulpit*, 84.

8. Spurgeon, *Metropolitan Tabernacle Pulpit*, 84.

9. J. Josh Smith, *The Titus Ten: Foundations for Godly Manhood* (B&H Publishing, 2022), 19–36.

Chapter 1

1. See "Evaluating Kings of Israel and Judah in 1-2 Kings," in *The ESV Global Study Bible* (Wheaton, IL: Crosssway, 2012), available from https://www.esv.org/resources/esv-study-bible/chart-11-02/.

2. Charles Spurgeon, *The Metropolitan Tabernacle Pulpit*, Volume 34 (Pilgrim Publications, 1974), 84.

3. Ray Pritchard, *Fire and Rain: The Wild-Hearted Faith of Elijah* (B&H Publishing, 2007), 26.

4. Dietrich Bonhoeffer, *The Cost of Discipleship* (Macmillan, 1963), 99.

Chapter 2

1. https://www.wholesomewords.org/missions/biotaylor2.html, accessed September 26, 2024

2. F. Howard Taylor and Geraldine Taylor, *Hudson Taylor's Spiritual Secret* (Moody, 1989), 23–24.

3. Taylor and Taylor, *Hudson Taylor's Spiritual Secret*, 32.

4. Eugene Peterson, *A Long Obedience in the Same Direction* (InterVarsity Press, 2000), 10.

5. https://thebensmartblog.com/2018/04/30/how-hudson-taylor-faced-unbearable-tragedies/

6. John Piper, *A Sweet and Bitter Providence* (Crossway, 2010), 101–2.

Chapter 3

1. David Powlison, "Sanctification Is a Direction," https://www.songtime.com/sanctification-is-a-direction-by-david-powlison/, accessed June 14, 2025.

2. Charles Spurgeon, *The Metropolitan Tabernacle Pulpit*, Volume 34 (Pilgrim Publications, 1974), 84.

Chapter 4

1. https://www.arunnathaniblog.com/the-brave-coward, accessed May 28, 2024.

2. Grant R. Osbourne, *Revelation*, Baker Exegetical Commentary (Baker, 2002), 742.

3. C. S. Lewis, *The Screwtape Letters* (New York, 1961), 137.

Chapter 5

1. Jonathan Edwards, *The Works of Jonathan Edwards* (The Banner of Truth Trust, 1998), xx–xxiii.

2. Edwards, *Works of Jonathan Edwards*, xx–xxiii.

3. Roger Ellsworth, *Standing for God: The Story of Elijah* (The Banner of Truth Trust, 1994), 54.

4. Randy Stinson and Dan Dumas, *A Guide to Biblical Manhood* (Southern Baptist Theological Seminary Press), 47.

5. Eugene Peterson, *A Long Obedience in the Same Direction* (InterVarsity Press, 2000), 10.

6. https://www.biblebb.com/files/spurgeon/3381.htm, accessed August 7, 2024

7. https://www.biblebb.com/files/spurgeon/3381.htm

8. Edwards, *Works of Jonathan Edwards*, xx–xxiii.

Chapter 6

1. Fred A. Hartley, *God on Fire* (CLC Publishers, 2012), 26.

2. William M. Taylor, *Elijah the Prophet* (Harper and Brothers, 1875), 92.

3. Bill Elliff, *The Presence Centered Church* (Graceful Truth, 2015), 13.

4. A. W. Tozer, *The Pursuit of God* (Moody, 2015), 41.

5. John Stott, *What Christ Thinks of the Church* (Baker, 1990), 113.

6. Bill Elliff, *The Presence Centered Church* (Grace and Truth Publications, 2015.

7. Tozer, *The Pursuit of God*, 41.

Chapter 7

1. Walter J. Chantry, *Today's Gospel: Authentic or Synthetic?* (Banner of Truth, 1970), 38–39.

2. Richard Owen Roberts, *Repentance: The First Word of the Gospel* (Crossway, 2002), 24–25.

3. Sinclair Furgeson, *The Grace of Repentance* (Crossway, 2010), 17.

Chapter 8

1. David Powlison, *Good and Angry* (New Growth, 2016), 9–22.

2. Powlison, *Good and Angry*, 104–6.

3. Powlison, *Good and Angry*, 112.

4. D. A. Carson, *The Gospel According to John*, The Pillar New Testament Commentary (Eerdmans,1991), 415–17.

5. Martyn Lloyd-Jones, *Darkness and Light* (Baker, 1982), 219.

6. https://www.desiringgod.org/interviews/does-righteous-anger-kill-our-joy#slow-to-anger, accessed June 6, 2024

Chapter 9

1. Paul E. Miller, *A Praying Life* (NavPress, 2009), 77–79.

2. Steve Gaines, *Pray Like It Matters* (Auxano, 2013), ix–xi.

3. E. M. Bounds, *The Complete Works of E. M. Bounds* (Baker, 1990), 447.

4. John Piper, *Let the Nations Be Glad* (Baker, 2003), 45.

5. Douglas J. Moo, *The Letter of James*, The Pillar New Testament Commentary (Apollos, 2000), 249.

6. George Müller and Roger Steer, *Spiritual Secrets of George Müller* (Harold Shaw Publishers, 1985), 59–61.

7. Fred Hartley, *Prayer on Fire* (NavPress, 2006), 20.

Chapter 10

1. Wayne Cordeiro, *Leading on Empty: Refilling Your Tank and Renewing Your Passion* (Bethany House, 2010), 13.

2. J. I. Packer, *Weakness Is the Way: Life with Christ Our Strength* (Crossway, 2013), 15–16.

About the Author

J. Josh Smith is the pastor of Prince Avenue Baptist Church, just outside of Athens, Georgia. He is the author of *The Titus Ten: Foundations for Godly Manhood.* He and his wife Andrea have four daughters and one son.

Also available from

J. Josh Smith